A POLISH VOICE

A POLISH VOICE

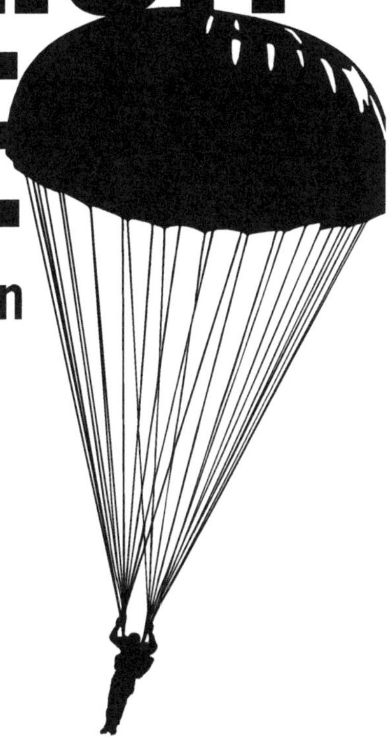

and my father, the man who always listened

Sandy Weatherburn

BROWN DOG BOOKS

First published 2023

Copyright © Sandy Weatherburn 2023

The right of Sandy Weatherburn to be identified as the author of this work has been asserted in accordance with the Copyright, Designs & Patents Act 1988.

All rights reserved. No part of this book may be reproduced, stored in a retrieval system, or transmitted in any form or by any means, electronic, electrostatic, magnetic tape, mechanical, photocopying, recording or otherwise, without the written permission of the copyright holder.

Published under licence by Brown Dog Books and
The Self-Publishing Partnership Ltd, 10b Greenway Farm, Bath Rd, Wick, nr. Bath BS30 5RL

www.selfpublishingpartnership.co.uk

ISBN printed book: 978-1-83952-615-2
ISBN e-book: 978-1-83952-616-9

Cover design by Kevin Rylands
Internal design by Andrew Easton

Printed and bound in the UK

This book is printed on FSC® certified paper

This book is dedicated to Laura, Emily, Jessica and William in memory of their grandfather and his Polish friend.

Contents

Dedication	5
Epigraph	8
Introduction	11
Chapter 1 – Early years in Poland	17
Chapter 2 – Prisoner of War and escape into the Ural Mountains	33
Chapter 3 – Meeting the British Army	57
Chapter 4 – Evacuation	74
Chapter 5 – Civilian life	113
Chapter 6 – Friendship in hospital	127
Memorials	133
Conclusion	137
References	141
Bibliography	142

'People disappear when they die. Their voice, their laughter, the warmth of their breath. Their flesh. Eventually their bones. All living memory of them ceases. This is both dreadful and natural. Yet for some there is an exception to this annihilation. For in the books they write they continue to exist. We can rediscover them. Their humour, their tone of voice, their moods. Through the written word they can anger you or make you happy. They can comfort you. They can perplex you. They can alter you. All this, even though they are dead. Like flies in amber, like corpses frozen in ice, that which according to the laws of nature should pass away is, by the miracle of ink on paper, preserved. It is a kind of magic.'

- Diane Setterfield, *The Thirteenth Tale*

'*Polish paratroopers could not have been more different. They were not like the British who just wanted to make the best of a bad war by joking and referring to any battle as "a party". Nor were they like the Americans who wanted to finish it quickly so that they could go home. The Poles were exiles, fighting for the very survival of their national identity. An American officer who saw them in training described them as "killers under the silk". Polish patriotism was nothing like the rather embarrassed British equivalent: theirs was a burning, spiritual flame.*'[i]

- Antony Beevor, *Arnhem: The Battle for the Bridges, 1944*

INTRODUCTION

This book is written as a tribute to the lives of Marian Jan Roguski and his friend Brian Neville Wilkins, who was my father. Both men's lives were affected by World War Two, but in completely different ways. Marian was born in Poland, Brian in England, and the differences in their circumstances and age made it unlikely that they would ever meet one another, but they did and without their chance meeting, this book would not exist. An incredible true story of the survival and determination of one Polish soldier, who survived captivity in Russia in 1940 and resisted it in Holland during 1944, was shared with Brian in a hospital bed in Bournemouth Hospital in 1995. Through the strangest of circumstances, this story has been left for me to tell, and to share with you. Their voices didn't die when their flesh did. I found them.

The research for writing this book began in February 2021 in the middle of the UK's third Coronavirus lockdown. If it were not for the lockdown situation, I do not believe that I would have found the time to write it, but I am gratified that I have done so as it has resulted in a permanent tribute to Marian Roguski's early life, a serving Polish soldier, who was one of thousands of young men who was separated from their families when World War Two broke out in Europe in 1939. It has also helped me to appreciate my father's life and accept his death by exploring how the war impacted his childhood.

The discovery of an old Dictaphone recorder led me to unravel a remarkable life of a young Polish soldier, and despite never meeting him, his voice has taken me on a journey into history, which has left me feeling humble and grateful for the knowledge that I have gained from hearing him speaking.

My dad, Brian Wilkins, died on 8 May 2020, aged 85. Sorting through his personal belongings has taken some time as he kept all sorts of paperwork associated with his long life. During a visit to see my mum, at her home in Weymouth in Dorset in February 2021, as her 'Covid support bubble carer', she handed me a box of Dad's personal letters and asked me to sort through them for her. Among many files of personal letters from friends and relatives was a blue cardboard folder, with the name MARION ROGUSKI (spelt incorrectly) written on the outside in blue marker pen. Inside this folder were several envelopes, including a large manilla one, which contained some small cassette tapes. I remembered that Dad had used a Dictaphone when he worked for Southern Electricity as a wayleave officer. He was employed by this organisation since leaving school, as he had hoped to join the Royal Navy, but failed the necessary entrance medical examination due to poor eyesight. He retired in 1992 but as he had always found the Dictaphone useful, when working outdoors recording important details of his visits, he had kept it.

During the year 1995 Dad was suddenly taken ill on his wedding anniversary, whilst on a short break to Jersey with Mum. He was initially treated at Jersey General Hospital in St Helier but was referred from the Channel Islands to the Royal Bournemouth Hospital on the mainland. Dad was transferred on a small plane with my mother and sister accompanying him. Andrea, my sister was studying nursing at Bournemouth University at the time and had rushed across the channel by ferry to support them both. Whilst receiving treatment for a thrombosis in the Royal Bournemouth Hospital, Dad struck up a friendship with a patient who was being treated in the same ward. The patient was Marian Jan Roguski. Dad was friendly towards most people as he always made an effort to talk to others, often in a jovial manner, making jokes and he smiled a lot. This chance meeting however, and the instant respect that Dad showed to Marian, led to Brian spending hours listening to his life story, as they both received treatment under the care of the National Health Service. Brian was discharged from the hospital before Marian but considered it so important to be able to remember his friend's story that he returned to the hospital ward as a visitor, on several occasions, to record Marian's voice at his bedside using his Dictaphone recorder. From his bed in Ward 22 of Bournemouth Hospital Marian recounted to Brian his incredible life story. These recordings have remained stored within the blue folder inside the manilla envelope ever since. I remembered Dad speaking about Marian, but as I was a mother to a two-year-old daughter at the time, I undoubtedly had limited interest in his conversations about the man in the bed next to him in hospital! Initially, I wondered what I should do with the small tapes and decided to ask Mum if she still had Dad's old Dictaphone, which she duly found. Once it was fitted with new batteries it sprang into life, and a more youthful sounding Dad, a voice that I was very familiar with, but had not heard for many years, emerged from the little machine. Not wanting to upset Mum by unexpectedly hearing her husband's voice, I swiftly made the decision to take the Dictaphone and the cassette tapes home and listen to them in private.

The recordings were quite clear, and I copied them onto digital recordings on my iPhone so that I could listen to them at my leisure. I heard the voice of Marian for the first time, a gentle and at times weak voice, with a strong Polish accent. Marian recounted some very personal details of his life, starting from when he was a young man and spoke about the outbreak of World War Two in his country, Poland in 1939. Marian spoke English well, but often found it difficult to find the right words for things that he was trying to describe, and at times he sounded quite feeble. Dad seemed to have taken on the role of a reporter, asking questions that prompted Marian to recount his life story. I listened to the recordings over several days, and my initial reaction was, that it all sounded a bit far-fetched and the events that Marian had recalled were probably fantasy. How wrong I was! I transcribed the tapes and wrote word for word what was recorded into several documents so that I could research his stories. During lockdown hours of 2021, I discovered that nearly everything that Marian had spoken of, could be backed up with facts and my interest in his life only intensified. I believe Dad had realised that Marian's life deserved to be recorded in a book and had at one time intended to ask someone to write it. He may have considered doing it himself, but during his own full and busy life, this never happened. Dad kept in contact with Marian and his wife, for several years, as some letters from them both were also contained in the blue folder. I could tell by reading these letters that Marian's health was in decline, and being quite a bit older than Dad, I was not surprised to read that he had died in 1998.

I felt compelled to write this book as an acknowledgement of their friendship. Whilst I never met Marian myself, I discovered that by listening to his voice, I became closely acquainted with a person from the past. I hope that you will find his life story as absorbing to read, as much as I have enjoyed writing about him, and in uncovering the life of a brave and resilient Polish serviceman, it is my hope that it is a small contribution to the history of persecuted Polish citizens who had no control over their future in 1939.

I have used Marian's story and the events that he and my father encountered during their young lives to weave historical wartime facts together, in order to give context and I have tried, in most instances, to do this chronologically. I also explain what happened to Marian after the war ended and why he never returned to his home in Poland. I hope that magically, as Diane Setterfield wrote in the quote at the beginning, that my dad's and Marian's characters and personalities are preserved by the '*miracle of ink on paper*' allowing their early life stories to be rediscovered.

I have asked myself this question and I have now proven that most of it is true. I have researched each part of Marian's life story and every aspect of it is linked to factual history. On 19 December 2021 I wrote to the Ministry of Defence, Army Personnel disclosures office at RAF Northolt in Ruislip to request details of Marian's military career. My enquiry was accepted but I did not receive a reply until August 2022. During this period, I was disheartened and began to wonder if some of Marian's recorded accounts were fabricated. However, when the envelope arrived at my home, on a hot August day, filled with copies of Marian's service history I was quite overwhelmed to be holding the evidence that would allow me to finish my book.

Major EW Rushton wrote a brief account of Marian's life in 1982 as he was acting on Marian's behalf by presenting his story to the Dorset War Pensions committee. He believed that Marian's life story was accurate and referred to it as '*epic, overflowing with courage, faith and dogged determination to be free and to play a full part not only in gaining freedom for himself but also willing to help others in their hopes to achieve the same for themselves*'. Major Rushton refers to the written work of Aleksandr Solzhenitsyn whose award-winning book *The Gulag Archipelago* is based on his own and other survivors' experiences of life in the Soviet Union's Gulag camps between 1918 and 1956. I have used this book as a reference point as well as Anne Applebaum's book *Gulag* (2004) and Jane Rogoyska's more detailed recent research in her book *Surviving Katyn*.

The facts relating to the beginning and end of World War Two, I have taken from various resources including *How The War Came* which is an extensively researched book written by Donald Cameron Watt. For a full list of sources that I have referred to during this research you will find in a bibliography at end of this book.

Initially, when writing Marian's memoir, I had doubts about the accuracy of the recounted stories that he shared with my dad in Bournemouth Hospital in 1995, and understand the credulity that he and many others felt on hearing Marian describe his experiences. Marian was not keen on sharing them at first, it was only my dad's ability to encourage him to open up and speak about them, that Marian's phenomenal early life history has been recorded. There are one or two discrepancies relating to the dates Marian joined the Polish Army. He claimed that he joined in 1938, but the records that I have managed to obtain state that he joined in 1942 in the Soviet Union. It is important to understand that there were several Polish armies during World War Two and it is likely that Marian joined a Warsaw-based legion. I have attempted to contact the Polish Military Records Office for further clarification of his service, but I have been unsuccessful. Many Polish service records were destroyed so this point is unproven, but whether he was imprisoned in Siberia as a Polish citizen or as a Polish soldier in 1940, the conditions would have been the same. I think it is only fair that we respect Marian's first-hand account of those conditions and accept that his recorded voice is all the evidence needed.

I have also asked myself the question, would Marian have wanted a book written about his life? That one I also cannot answer. But I **have** written one, and I have absolutely no reason to disbelieve anything that Marian told Brian.

CHAPTER 1

The beginning of World War Two impacted both Brian and Marian's early lives in different ways. Marian was a teenager and Brian a young child when Germany invaded Poland in September 1939. This first chapter introduces these young men. Their age differences and their countries of birth meant that their experiences were very different, but on meeting 56 years later, they were united by the memories of the trauma of war.

Marian Jan Roguski was born in Poland on 11 February 1922, 50 miles east of Warsaw, in a small village called Kopcie, within the county of Siedlce. His parents were Josef and Stephania, and they lived on a family run farm. Marian had two siblings, one brother and one sister. Marian was christened and brought up within a Roman Catholic household.

The second Republic of Poland was reformed as an independent country in 1918 after being partitioned for over 100 years of territorial disagreements by the Austrian-Hungary, German and Russian Empires. A war between Poland and Vladimir Lenin's Bolshevik regime culminated in August 1920 when Marshal Józef Piłsudski prevented the Red Army[1] from gaining control of the capital city during 'The Battle of Warsaw'. Poland had pleaded for help from western countries and the British Prime Minister David Lloyd George told his government that the country would have to accept its fate. Pope Benedict XV implored that prayers should be said for Poland as a defeat to the Red Army was expected. Piłsudski's ingenious tactics saw thousands of Soviet troops killed on the banks of the Vistula River which became known historically as 'The Miracle on the Vistula'. His actions defeated Lenin's troops, saved Warsaw from complete

---

1 Red Army (Krasnaya Armiya) was the Soviet Army created after the Bolshevik Revolution of 1917. Marshal of Poland is the highest rank in the Polish Army.

catastrophe and prevented communism spreading into Europe. 'The Treaty of Riga (1921)', a declaration of peace, was signed on 18 March in Latvia, which defined the mutual border of the two countries, giving Poland parts of Belorussia (now Belarus).

However, Piłsudski's confidence, gained from defeating the Soviet Union, was responsible for Poland's belief that they could also maintain victory over Germany in 1939, without the support of the Soviet Union. This optimism was ultimately a catastrophe for Poland as Germany's occupation during World War Two enticed Adolf Hitler into a war with the Soviet Union which eventually annihilated him and his country.

When Marian was a baby in 1922, Poland's frontiers had only just been recognised under the terms of another peace treaty, the Treaty of Versailles.[2] The country did not maintain a democracy for many years, as during 1926 a military coup brought this to an end. A large proportion of the country was made up of people with different ethnic backgrounds including Jews, Germans, Belarusians, Lithuanians and Ukrainians. Poland was beset with social and economic difficulties with minority ethnicities becoming marginalised due different religious beliefs and social differences. During these same years the Russian Empire transformed into the communist state of the Union of Soviet Socialist Republics (USSR), after a civil war, leading to the rise of power to the Bolshevik political party.

In September 1939, when the war began, around 50 per cent of Siedlce's residents were Jewish. Siedlce was occupied by German troops from October, and the Nazis systematically began to arrest Jews and imprisoned them in the Siedlce Ghetto, a prison camp where thousands of Jews from many other parts of Poland were rounded up and kept in appalling conditions. Using propaganda, the Nazis justified their murder by claiming that typhus spread more quickly amongst Jewish

---

2 The Treaty of Versailles was signed on 28 June 1919 in the Place of Versailles in France, but was not registered until 21 October 1919. This brought World War One to an official end although the fighting had ended with an armistice on 11 November 1918.

people. Many people who were detained here were later deported to Treblinka extermination camp, which opened in 1942, and was located in a forest 2.5 miles north of Warsaw.

Marian would have been 12 years old when Brian was born in Weymouth, Dorset, England on 6 June 1934. Brian was the eldest son of Ida and William Wilkins. Brian was also christened as a baby, but unlike Marian whose family followed the Roman Catholic faith, Brian's family observed the teachings of the Church of England. Brian's father, William's ancestors had moved to Weymouth from Odstock near Salisbury seeking higher paid employment than they received as farm workers, and his great grandfather John William Wilkins was successful in finding employment with Devenish Brewery, becoming the landlord of The Globe Inn, Weymouth in 1880.

William Wilkins, who was born on 20 August 1904, grew up with two younger sisters at 2, New Close Gardens in Weymouth. As a young man he became the proud owner of a motorbike and worked as a mechanic at Bell's Garage in Franchise Street. He hoped to run his own garage business but failed to get permission to develop a plot of land in Sudan Road for this purpose. This was a disappointment to him, but he changed direction and initially worked at the Whiteheads torpedo factory before moving to the Ministry of Defence torpedo base at Bincleaves in Weymouth as a Chargeman of Fitters.

During the 1930s, in Britain, there were several changes to both the monarchy and to the government. Most British people were keen to avoid another world war, as families had not come to terms with the devastation and grief associated with the loss life in World War One. It was a positive time for Brian's parents, who had fallen in love, married on 28 December 1931 and moved into a family home together: 'St Helier', 7 Clearmount Road, Weymouth.

Brian's mother Ida Winifred (née Collins) had grown up with her four siblings in a house in Glen Avenue and she was very nearly a victim of diphtheria. This acute bacterial infection predominately affected children under the age of five. Before a vaccination programme was introduced in Britain in the 1920s, the only treatment was a surgical tracheotomy, allowing air to reach the lungs as the symptoms of the illness caused the child's airway to become blocked. Ida was treated in an isolation hospital in Chickerell, where she recovered, but the long-term effects of this illness left her with hearing problems.

William and Ida became parents and named their son Brian Neville Wilkins. Dad hated his middle name, but it was chosen as it was familiar to his parents, being the name of the Conservative Member of Parliament, Neville Chamberlain, who was elected as Prime Minister in May 1937. Dad told me that he was probably lucky to have been given the name Brian, as he thought that his parents had considered calling him Windsor, as a racehorse called Windsor Lad won the prestigious Epsom Derby horse race around the time that Brian was born. Ida was challenged with her hearing difficulties and had difficulty breastfeeding Brian so had to use the services of a wet nurse. This was a woman who suckled another person's child, which was a reliable practice, used before the invention of formula milk. At some point in Brian's early childhood, he was fed milk that was infected with a pathogenic bacterium. Bovine tuberculosis was controlled in Great Britain, at this time, by herd testing and the introduction of pasteurisation in the 1930s, but the milk that Brian's mother obtained from a local farm was not put through either of these safeguarding processes. Ida, like any mother wanting to nurture their child, gave him the farm milk, in ignorance that it would cause him any harm, and it didn't until he was a father himself, when he became seriously ill with a kidney infection linked to tuberculosis during the 1960s.

King George V who had reigned throughout World War One, began the Royal tradition of Christmas broadcasts in 1932, and in 1935, one year after Brian's birth he celebrated his Silver Jubilee, which probably contributed to the patriotism of the Wilkins family. My childhood memories of Christmas celebrations always included my dad insisting that we should listen to Her Majesty the Queen on Christmas Day, which would have originally been transmitted from Sandringham via 'wireless' (as radio was referred to then). King George V died shortly after his last Christmas broadcast in January 1936. He was succeeded by his eldest son Edward VIII, who was only King for a year due to his decision to abdicate, so that he could marry an American divorcee, Wallis Simpson. George V's second son Prince Albert then became King George VI in December 1936.

The day after Brian's 1st birthday the Conservative Party leader Stanley Baldwin became Prime Minister. He had served in this role on two previous occasions, beating Labour's Ramsay MacDonald in the 1935 general election with a large majority vote.

The Wilkins family lived at number 7 Clearmount Road in Weymouth. Like many families, they grew fruit and vegetables in their garden, to help feed themselves. Brian's father William also enjoyed fishing and the family enjoyed living by the seaside. In May 1937 Chamberlain succeeded Baldwin as the Conservative Prime Minister. Chamberlain was dedicated to preventing any further conflict in Europe and met with Hitler in 1938 to discuss resolutions that he hoped would ensure peace. However, in the spring of 1939 he made some preparations for war by introducing the Military Training Act of 1939 forcing young men aged between 20 and 22 to register for six months' military training.

When Chamberlain's efforts for peace failed, with Nazi Germany invading Poland, Britain declared war and The National Service (Armed Forces) Act of 1939 declared that all males aged between 18 and 41 were legally required to register for service for their country. William Wilkins would have been 37, but he was considered exempt due to his engineering work in the torpedo factory, which was deemed essential. William did become a member of the Home Guard, which was operational as citizen military support from 1940 until 1944.

Brian's earliest memories, therefore, would have been as five-year-old boy, as the war started in 1939. His memories of this time were from a younger child's perspective than his friend Marian who was aged 17. This age difference is important to appreciate as Marian's recorded tale unfolds.

At the beginning of the recorded tapes, Marian told Brian that he remembered his father had instructed him to learn construction skills, which he referred to as 'brickware', when he was aged 15. Marian said that he hadn't enjoyed that work very much and it sounded as though he was an ambitious teenager who was keen to leave home and explore the world. As a younger child he had helped with work on his family's farm, milking cows by hand. Marian did work in the building trade for a while, before joining the Polish Army in 1938. He would have been 16 years old at this time, and said he was accepted into the Army, joining Thirty-Six Company.[3]

The influences on his early life would have been mostly family based, and how much knowledge he had of the political state of his country at this time would have depended on what his parents had told him. He did not speak of school at all. Naivety may have been a blessing, as Polish families' lives were all threatened by the Russian leader Joseph Stalin, as an exhibition in September 2019 revealed. This event, which was held in a cathedral in Odessa, Ukraine, was organised by Poland's Institute of National Remembrance and it addressed the **'The Polish Operation'**, a genocide involving hundreds of thousands of Polish citizens who were killed under the orders of the Soviet leader Stalin. The aim of the exhibition was to increase awareness of the massacre that had been led by Soviet Secret Police official, Nikolai Yezhov. Amongst the displays of photographs and documents was a typewritten memo signed by Yezhov stating that 'the Poles should be completely destroyed'.[ii] Stalin accused Polish men of espionage, and

---

3 This regiment was formed in 1918, made up of volunteer students from Warsaw universities. During 1939 the 'Thirty-Sixth Infantry Regiment' became part of the Prusy Army, formerly called the Warszawa Army.

ordered that over 100,000 were to be killed, with many being shot in the back of the head. A second order from Yezhov instructed that the wives and children of the murdered men be deported to Kazakhstan. As the horrors of this massacre were not common knowledge until this 2019 exhibition portrayed them publicly, Marian would, thankfully, have been unaware of these atrocities that were being committed against Poland's citizens at the same time that he was signing up for service in the Polish Army.

During Marian's first month of Army service, he worked in a familiar environment, with animals, but sounded rather unimpressed by his responsibilities, when sharing his memories with Brian. 'I only fed the bloomin' horses and a cow,' he complained, but sounded a lot more excited about prospects of becoming a proper soldier, after he had finished his training. In 1939 he was sent to fight the Germans when war broke out in Poland. Inexperienced, young, innocent soldiers at this time could never have imagined what atrocities were ahead and would have had no idea of how their lives would be changed forever. Knowledge of their country's politics and that of other countries around them after World War One would have been dependant on their education and attentiveness to news that reached their young ears. Marian, like most young men of his age was eager to leave his childhood behind, to become a soldier.

Communism and Nazism emerged after World War One, which saw Soviet Russia and other European countries developing their ideas of totalitarian social order. The beliefs that one human race was superior to another were being impregnated into young people's minds as they looked to their elders and educators for adult guidance. Most parents shelter their children from rumours of evil human behaviour and presuming Josef and Stephania had behaved in this way, Marian would have been protected from learning about the vile dehumanisation process that was occurring in Soviet and Nazi concentration camps during his childhood years. People were being incarcerated in these types of prison camps for who they were, for their ethnicity, not for what they had done wrong.

German troops began invading Poland on 1 September 1939, triggering the response from Britain and France to declare war on Nazi Germany. Earlier in the year the German dictator, Hitler was intent on invading Poland and had previously made preliminary steps in the form of international antagonistic propaganda. 'Operation Himmler' was a campaign that aimed to make it appear that Poland was being aggressive towards Germany. This strategy was conceived by Heinrich Himmler, a leading member of the Nazi Party, who accused the Polish government of condoning ruthless ethnic cleansing of citizens living in Poland who had descended from German ancestors. It was this false claim that resulted in Germany claiming they had justification for the decision to invade Poland. During the Nuremberg Trials many years later, information was revealed detailing how German radio operators disguised themselves as Polish officials. The deception gave them the opportunity to hijack the Gleiwitz radio station and to broadcast a message in Polish that was inflammatory, requesting that Polish citizens living in Germany should revolt against Hitler. To make this Machiavellian attack appear to be authentic, Franciszek Honik a Polish

Catholic farmer, was murdered and his body was used as part of the enactment at the radio station. Honik is considered to be the first victim of World War Two.

In August of that same year the foreign secretaries of Germany and the Soviet Union signed a non-aggression pact and agreed secretly that the country of Poland should be dissected and divided up between them, with Germany taking the western third and the Soviet Union taking the eastern two thirds. This is known as the Molotov–Ribbentrop Pact.

The invasion on 1 September 1939, referred to as Fall Weiss, was a tactical plan to invade Poland simultaneously from three directions. The main aerial attack took place at dawn on the western border of Poland from East Germany. In the north, the city of Danzig was attacked with bombs directed at both civilian and military targets.[4] In the early hours of the same day German troops aboard their battleship Schleswig-Holstein opened fire on the Polish resistance garrison of the Westerplatte, coinciding with the aerial attack by Stuka bombers.

From the south, German troops advanced through Slovakia. The three planned invasion commands were expected to converge on Warsaw where they were ordered to encircle the Polish troops. German forces used tanks on the ground which were called 'Panzerkampfwagen' who became known as Panzer troops. They very quickly overwhelmed the less equipped Polish soldiers despite a brave resistance led by Colonel Sosabowski. The Panzer troops were supported by air attacks from the German Luftwaffe who gained air superiority, rapidly forcing the Poles to retreat, and Sosabowski was proud of the efforts of his calvary units who were resilient despite being the weaker army.

On 3 September the UK and France declared war on Germany in

---

4 Danzig is the German name for Gdansk, an ancient city that was founded in the 10th century. The Free City of Danzig was created in 1920 after World War One as part of the Treaty of Versailles, and was then protected by the League of Nations, an international diplomacy group, which preceded the United Nations. The area surrounding Danzig was mostly inhabited by Germans, but the Polish had certain communication rights and access to the port and to the railway.

response to their actions against Poland. The Polish Army subsequently tried to counterattack the German forces in the Battle of Bzura, which took place between 9 and 19 September, named due to battle's location near the Bzura River, but has been referred to as bloody and bitter battle.

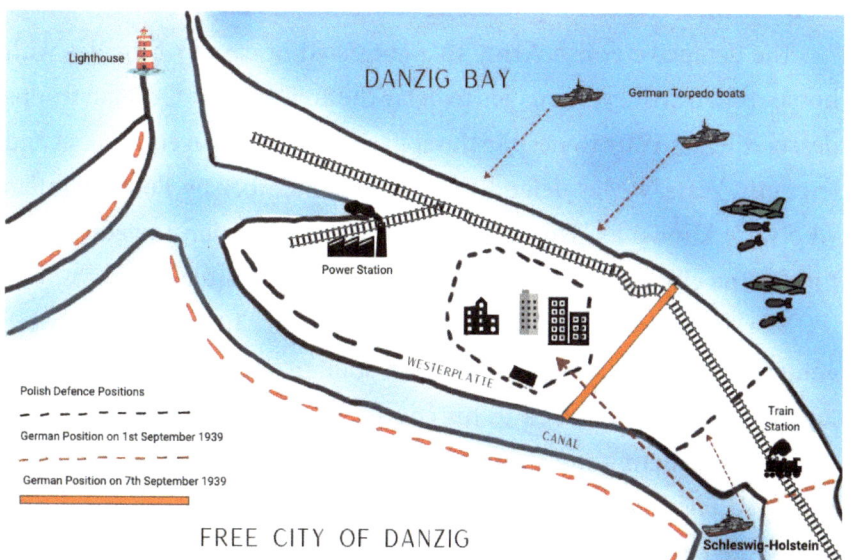

Schleswig-Holstein and Westerplatte

The Soviet invasion of Poland from the east began on 17 September 1939 and after only 20 days of military operations the two invading countries were occupying their previously agreed zones. Poland was attacked from both sides and sustained heavy defeats in battle. The Soviet Union also took control of the armies of Estonia, Latvia and Lithuania, known collectively the Baltic States. Thousands of Polish military were taken as prisoners of war by Soviet Russia's NKVD (law enforcement organisation) and many were murdered after they surrendered.

The President of the Polish Republic at this time was Ignacy Mościciki, who was trying to remain safe in the town of Kuty (now in Ukraine). On 17 September he issued a proclamation to transfer his power and appointed Władysław Rackiewicz to become his successor. At the end of the month Mościciki resigned and Rackiewicz took the oath to become his successor in Paris, where he appointed Władysław to be his Prime Minister of the government operating in exile. The Polish Navy moved their base to Scotland, berthing their ships in the harbours of Leith, Rosyth, Port Glasgow, Greenock and Dundee, commencing their wartime relationship working alongside the Royal Navy.

The defensive Polish Army that consisted of cavalry brigades with horse-drawn artillery managed to delay the arrival of the German troops descending on Warsaw despite the apparent weakness in equipment and strength. Warsaw was defended until 30 September by Polish fighters who were known as 'The children of Warsaw'. Civilian tragedies were high as the city was under siege until inevitable capitulation.

Marian told Brian that the German soldiers he had fought were equipped with tanks, whilst the Polish soldiers only had horses. In the tape recording he referred to his commanding officer as being a 'silly fool' for instructing the young soldiers that they must fight the better equipped enemy. History records estimate that 20,000 Polish soldiers were killed in this battle along with 8,000 German troops. George Cholewczynski, in his excellent book *Poles Apart,* writes that 40,000 of Warsaw's citizens were killed in the siege.[iii] It is not surprising to hear that Marian was keen to withdraw from the fighting at the earliest opportunity and he told Brian that his commanding officer threatened to shoot him if he did not obey orders. He must have been a terrified young man but was bold enough to give him an obstinate reply. Marian said he retorted: 'what difference will it make if you shoot me or the Germans?' One can easily understand how Marian's cheeky comment might have contributed to a change of heart by the equally frantic officer. Polish soldiers did have reputation for good discipline, but this type of retort is understandable in their desperate situation.

Marian went on to describe how his battalion, 36 Company, withdrew to the vicinity of the Romanian Border. He conveyed his memories of how he and his Polish military comrades travelled on foot and by train, leaving the horses behind, to set up camp on the border where further fighting broke out between both German and Soviet soldiers. Marian remembered that a lot of German soldiers were killed there. In his own words he said:

'*'nother ones, Russian fighting, Russia start coming, Russian soldiers, we said blimey we have two armies fighting one against another.*'

The Polish Army's plan was to prolong defence until the British and French could provide support, but it never came. The planned French 'Saar Offensive' was ineffective in its mobilisation the term 'Phoney War' was conceived. This term describes eight months when very little warfare involving Britain and France took place. On 17 September the Soviet Union violated the Molotov–Ribbentrop Pact and attacked Poland on the pretext that they were protecting Belarusian and Ukrainian citizens. This aggression, when 8,000 Red Army soldiers entered Poland, is the moment that Marian described. The Polish Army knew that they were overpowered. There was a huge loss of life in the fighting between the Russian, German and Polish soldiers, with Polish troops being taken captive by the Soviet Union as prisoners of war.

More than 13 million Polish citizens were then subject to a reign of terror after the beginning of the brutal Nazi regime and faced displacement from their country, starvation and mass executions in concentration camps.

Thousands of servicemen who were arrested by the Soviet Union, including Marian, never got to see their families again. Marian's early years, growing up and working with his parents on their farm in Kopcie, was the only time in his life when he spent time with his blood relatives. I don't think Marian had spoken about his family for many years when Brian asked him to talk about them in Ward 22 of Bournemouth Hospital 56 years later. Dad was always good at listening to people and always took genuine interest in them and I know that he would be pleased that Marian's story is finally being told. The personal information that Marian shared with Brian in hospital has allowed me to piece together what happened after he was captured as a prisoner of war. Marian's recorded accounts of his memories of the beginning of the Polish Holocaust give a real insight into how a generation of children's and teenagers' lives were dominated by the atrocities of the war.

It is important to understand that between the two World Wars the Polish government had not been at all stable. The Second Polish Republic established its independence in 1918 and it was a country that had been reborn after many years of partitioning. The population was made up of a mixture of minority groups from various native origins and the country had major economic problems. Due to the social issues caused by these factors there were several active opposition political parties trying to meet secretly in Warsaw at the beginning of the World War Two, risking their lives, due to political activities that were forbidden under German Nazi control. Two secret Polish military organisations emerged. One of these was the Secret Army whose principles stood by the 'two enemies doctrine' which was a declaration of hostility towards both Nazi Germany and to Soviet Russia. It was formed in the war office in Pilsudski Square, Warsaw at the end of September 1939 under the authority of General Juliusz Rommel, who appointed Michał Karaszewicz-Tokarzewski to command it. Shortly after this meeting the building was destroyed by the German military, and Rommel fled to Romania. Tokarzewski promised that he would take the responsibility for preparing and organising underground armed resistance when it was ordered for him to do so. By December 1939 he had managed to set up a secret military structure in the German and Soviet occupied zones of Poland. General Tokarzewski named the secret army 'Service for Polish Victory' (SFPV) and had no problem in recruiting young enthusiastic soldiers. He also sought the support of the political parties that were opposed to the Polish government before the outbreak of war.

Meanwhile, the new Polish parliament that was based in Paris, led by Prime Minister Sikorski, was also planning the formation of a parallel underground army using thousands of troops that were displaced in Europe, to form the 'Union for Armed Struggle' (UFAS) as part of the

Polish Armed Forces. He commanded that this should be the only secret army operating in Poland, and that any other groups should be subservient to it. General Kazimierz Sosnkowski was appointed as chief commander. A meeting between the leaders of the two organisations on 26 February 1940 agreed that they should become linked and that the SFVP be subordinate to UFAS.

Marian knew that his father's life had ended in 1939 but did not give Brian any details of how he had died, and he might not even have known, the only word he used when speaking about this was '*bomb*', so I assume he was killed in a bomb blast.

Warsaw, the capital city of Poland, was under attack for the whole of the month of September 1939 from the German Wehrmacht. The Polish army did not receive any support from their western allies so they defended the city as best they could, but with constant air attacks from the Luftwaffe, 40 per cent of the city was bombed. The city was under siege, with no access to food or medical supplies, the civilian casualties are recorded as numbering in the region of 180,000. Kopcie, where the Roguski family lived was on the outskirts of Warsaw, so until the fighting stopped on 29 September 1939, when a ceasefire was agreed, the family would have lived in daily fear of being taken prisoners or being killed. When the capitulation of Warsaw was agreed at the end of September, 140,000 Polish troops were taken as German prisoners of war.

Marian believed that his brother, Janik, had died in the Battle of Britain in 1940 and claimed that he was a Spitfire pilot. Polish airmen made up the largest part of non-British personnel involved in this operation. Winston Churchill referred to all the pilots who took part as 'The Few', which came from the words of his famous speech given on 20 August 1940, when he said:

'Never in the field of human conflict, was so much owed by so many to so few'.

The British Royal Air Force discovered that the Poles had very good combat experience and many exiled servicemen were accepted into RAF squadrons in Britain.

Marian also talked about his brother evacuating his wife and a son to London in a Polish plane, but said, tragically they too were killed in bomb blast in a hotel, three weeks after Janik had been killed. I am not at all surprised that Marian did not want to speak much about these terrible times, as far as I am able to establish, every single member of his family was killed during the war.

I could not find his brother's name on the wall of the national Battle of Britain Memorial at Capel-le-Ferne, Folkestone, Kent, or on the definitive list of airmen on the Battle of Britain London Monument, so it would appear that Janik was not an airman at this time.

Marian's mother and sister died later in 1944 during the Warsaw Uprising. Marian told Brian that they were both killed by a bomb, but he did not reveal any more details, and this may have been too painful for him to discuss. In Chapter 4 I have written more about the efforts of the Polish resistance to defend Warsaw at this time.

I have tried extensively to locate records of Marian's parents' and siblings' deaths and any associated military service but have been unable to find out any further details and have no way of finding out any more information. I wrote to the military records office in Warsaw but did not get a reply. The name 'Josef Roguski' is engraved on a memorial in Warsaw, with the date of death recorded as 1939, but I cannot prove that it was Marian's father. I would like to think that this book will become a lasting tribute to Marian's contribution as a Polish soldier and to any of the Roguski family that died as a consequence of World War Two.

CHAPTER 2

In Chapter 1, I have given as much information as I could find out about Marian's early life and explained how he grew up in a small town near Warsaw. I knew a little more about Brian's early childhood years as I was able to talk to his younger sister Rosemary, who was born in 1940. Brian and his sister were brought up with extended family living nearby as their grandparents owned a house in New Close Gardens in Weymouth. Brian had another sister Margaret, who was born later in 1949.[5]

Most children do not remember much about their lives before they are about four or five so the start of World War Two would not have had such an impact on Brian as it did on Marian, who in comparison was separated from his family as soon as the war in Poland broke out in September 1939. But as Brian became old enough to start attending school, the war did affect his childhood, which I will explain in more detail as this book unfolds.

Moving into this second chapter, the account of the traumatic experiences, that Marian experienced and shared with Brian in Bournemouth Hospital, give a detailed insight into how he became one of the thousands of Polish soldiers that were captured in the east of Poland by the Soviet Union and taken as prisoners of war. Marian's young life could so easily have ended at this point, as numerous Polish soldiers were killed immediately after their capture, suffering barbaric deaths, with many being shot in the back of their heads and buried in mass graves.

Marian's own descriptions of his capture and of his experiences of incarceration in the Soviet Union and Siberia in late 1939 until the beginning of 1940, describe bleak and freezing conditions which he

---

5 Margaret died in December 2021.

somehow managed to survive. His own voice, which I found on Brian's Dictaphone tapes in 2020, has helped me to research the account of an exceptional story of survival and resilience. Marian never mentioned feeling frightened, he only seemed to want to share with Brian his remarkable true life story and appeared grateful that he had found someone who would listen and understand what it meant to be Polish during the war. His ingenuity and determination to remain alive through resourcefulness and stamina, highlights the sharp-wittedness of Marian's character.

I have not been able to establish exactly which prison camp Marian was held at as there were so many labour camps. *'By the end of September, the Red Army held 230,000 Polish soldiers and officers in captivity. Many were released, particularly younger soldiers of lower rank, although some – those considered potential partisans – eventually made their way either into the Gulag, or into one of the hundred or so POW camps deeper in the USSR'*.[iv] Marian's explanations, however, did help me establish that he was held in a forest labour camp, and through researching other soldiers' experiences, I have been able to make informed suggestions as to where he was held.

If Marian had been a higher-ranking soldier, he would likely have become one of the 20,000 captured Polish officers that went missing in the Soviet Union in the early part of 1940, secretly, brutally murdered by the Soviet authorities.

In order to understand Marian's situation at this time, it is necessary for you, the reader, to appreciate the historical circumstances of 1939. Imperial Russia became Soviet Russia in 1917 when Vladimir Lenin became leader. His radical Marxist influenced beliefs, led to the development of concentration camps. Lenin was the head of Soviet Russia until his death in 1924 and he was responsible for the development of a type of communism, that is referred to as Leninism, which was based on the ideas of philosophers Karl Marx and Friedrich Engels. Lenin wanted to create a community in which all citizens worked for the benefit of the state. In order to do this, he needed to destroy the pre-existing capitalist society, that had operated in Imperial Russia, under the control of the Tsars. Under this new regime a criminal would have been defined as an enemy of the state, usually because of their class or their political principles.

From 1918, until the year before Marian's birth in 1922, violent civil war swept across the Russian countryside. Leon Trotsky was appointed Commissar of War by Lenin, leading the Red Army to victory over disunited battalions of counterrevolutionary groups known as the White Army. Under the communist rule of Lenin, a network of detention centres evolved. These forced labour camps were interspersed across the whole of the Soviet Union and Siberia. Lenin's leadership was supported by his own secret police known as the Cheka. These secret police officers had authority to arrest anyone who was considered to be a criminal, and labour camps were created to detain and punish the bourgeois citizens who fell into this category of criminality purely because of their class or Imperial background. These type of labour camps became known as 'gulags' but were not referred to as such until 1930 under the Soviet Union's subsequent ruler Stalin. GULAG is an acronym from the Russian words that translates to 'Main Camp Administration', but the word 'gulag' has evolved to not only describe the management of these camps, but also the structure of the Soviet Union's regime of slavery and repression over its population, beginning in 1917, during the Russian Revolution.

Before World War Two Stalin had introduced a five-year plan to industrialise the Soviet Union rapidly. He undertook a process referred to as 'collectivisation' ordering all Soviet farms to become a 'Kolkhozes'.[6] During a period in 1937, referred to as 'The Great Purge', Stalin ordered ruthless ethnic cleansing, targeting the Kulaks,[7] by murdering them or

---

6 Kolkhozes were state-owned farms.

7 Kulaks were farming people who owned land.

committing them to exile in forced labour camps. Anyone living in the Soviet Union at that time was at risk of being arrested.

Stalin's idea was that all who were put into prison camps would become the labour force that would speed up his industrialisation programme. 'The Great Purge' was led by Soviet state security, which had evolved from Lenin's 'Cheka' to become the 'NKVD'.[8]

When Marian was captured 1939, Stalin's agricultural 'collectivisation programme' meant that Russian farming communities suffered from food shortages, as the crops were taken by the state, so thousands of people were already starving when they were arrested. Factual accounts recorded by people who were imprisoned in the gulag camps, tell of continued interrogation by the NKVD, who operated programmes of torture. Vera Shultz recorded in her memoirs details of her own incarceration in the gulag system, and wrote, *'It seemed as if the monstrous Stalinist regime had given birth to a new type of human being'*, and she wanted later generations of women to understand the dehumanisation process that she had experienced in the camps. She spoke of *'the nightmare of false accusation, torture, humiliation, hunger, and unspeakable deprivation'*.[v] One of these methods of torture used by the NKVD was not allowing prisoners to go to sleep during the night and keeping them working for days at time until they collapsed with exhaustion. They would then be deemed unsuitable for work so would be executed.

Under Stalin's orders, prisoners in the most northern and uninhabited parts of the Soviet Union were forced to dig the Belomorkanal,[9] mine for coal and supply timber in forest processing camps. Marian spoke a little about being tortured and said that he never trusted anything that the Soviet soldiers said to him. He mentioned being interrogated by a woman and having to sit in a special chair. She asked him to reveal

---

8 NKVD translates to People's Commissariat for Internal Affairs, a secret police force that oversaw the running of the gulag camps.

9 Belomorkanal is the White Sea Canal.

who was an officer in the Polish Army. He did not know then that the fate of many imprisoned Polish officers would become one of the worst atrocities of the war.

Four thousand Polish officers, who should have been protected by the 1929 Geneva Convention POW legislation,[10] were detained in three different prison camps at Kozelsk, Starobilsk and Ostashkov, were selected for extermination on orders from Stalin and were shot in the backs of their heads and buried secretly in the Katyn Forest, several months later in May 1940. This shocking genocide[11] was carried out secretly by the NKVD and was not discovered until 1943, when the Soviet Union tried to lay blame on Germany for carrying out the murders. The Soviet Union's intensive industrialisation programme, under Stalin's leadership, made the country 'the second greatest industrial Power in the World'.[vi]

Anne Applebaum explains in her book *Gulag* that there were records of 476 different prison camps, but some of these camps were complexes, containing other smaller camps. The Soviet Union's prison camp system also included special prisoner of war exile camps, which is the type that Marian was held in. Gulags tended to be surrounded with barbed wire fences and watchtowers, but they varied considerably in construction.

As I have explained, all Polish citizens were subject to the risk of arrest and internment in a forced labour camp, it was not just the soldiers who were sent to them. These camps were bestrewn throughout the country. People were transferred to them by train and on foot. Aleksandr Solzhenitsyn, who was sentenced to work in coal mines at a forced labour camp in Ekibastus in Kazakhstan, wrote about these types of journeys

---

10 A series of international treaties developed in association with the Red Cross that establish legal standards for humanitarian law.

11 The word 'genocide' was not used until 1944 but was adopted in 1948 by the United Nations Genocide Convention as an international treaty. It is defined as 'acts committed with intent to destroy, in whole or in part, a national, ethnic, racial or religious group'.

in his book *The Gulag Archipelago*. He recorded that small fires were lit inside animal trucks for the purpose of lighting the trains, rather than heating them.[vii] The passengers were unloaded in very low temperatures that were 32ºC below zero. Solzhenitsyn served a 12-year sentence in the camp at Ekibastus and remained in exile working as a teacher. Later, he wrote many acclaimed literary books and a successful play, which denounced Stalin's crimes, and he is considered to be one of the most important Russian writers who revealed to the world the regime and systems of terror that operated in the Soviet Union at that time.

Lavrentiy Beria, the chief of the Soviet state security ordered the NKVD to manage the Polish prisoners of war. After being captured by the Red Army, the prisoners were then handed to them to be transferred by rail to one of the network of camps. A department of the NKVD was formed dedicated to the handling of prisoners of war and other detained foreign civilians. The camps that were created for these detainees had the same function as the gulags, being forced labour, and whilst the camps were similar there were nuances in their administration.

Captured Polish soldiers, including Marian, were loaded into animal trucks on Polish trains. He recalled the noises of men crying, and shared with Brian memories of feeling very cold. The prisoners were then transferred from the Polish train onto a larger one, as they travelled into Soviet Russia. It was during this transfer that Marian remembered having his hands inspected. He believed that his captors were trying to establish if the men had good working hands and described this to Brian in his own words:

'Officer tries looking if blisters in the hands, working hands you go on the right, if you anything there you go on the left,'.

Speaking about this triggered Marian's memory of a Polish officer being killed there by the Soviet soldiers, because his hands were too delicate and not rough. Marian, having worked on his parents' farm doing manual work, presumably had rather rough skin on his hands, which indicated he was used to manual labour. The soldiers who had passed the 'hand test' qualified to live! Marian's rough working hands gave him eligibility to board the next train, which he remembered had travelled deep into the Russian countryside for several days. Brian wondered if Marian was still wearing a uniform or if it had been taken away from him. Marian told him:

'I still got a uniform, Polish uniform'.

Marian remembered being transported on a train, squashed into a cattle truck, which headed north, taking him and the other Polish prisoners of war to Moscow, where Marian said that he was given something to eat. Average temperatures in Moscow in October are between eight and two degrees Celsius, so his journey on the train would have been extremely cold and miserable. Marian's voice, on the recorded tapes, is very weak at times and understanding everything that he had to say was challenging. Recounting his journey to Brian, when he was lying in a hospital bed in 1995, feeling unwell, was probably not an easy task for him, but he remembered that the journey had been extremely uncomfortable. He spoke about how the train stopped sometimes so that the prisoners could dig holes in the snow for toileting purposes. The animal trucks were cramped and dark, and any men who became unwell were thrown out and left to die in the cold. A Polish family who were transported, after their arrest, on this same train route in 1940 describe the cattle trains: *'There was a hole cut in on the train, so everyone did their toilet business there in front of the entire crowd. Among the crowd there were the sickly, the elderly, young people, and middle-aged people. Not only was it crowded, uncomfortable, and dirty, they had to travel to their mysterious destination in the severe cold and blistering blizzards'*[viii]

Marian would have passed Griazovets, which is 250 miles north of Moscow, where a former Orthodox convent was converted into a prison camp for 395 Polish officers during 1940. If you were to travel to Griazovets, by train today, from Moscow, it would take about nine hours, but it would have been a far slower journey in 1939 as Marian would have been a travelling on a steam train. There are accounts of Polish survivors, who remembered being on trains for nearly three weeks, as they travelled between different detention camps.

Józef Czapski was a reserve officer with the Polish Army and was one of the officers to be imprisoned at the Griazovets camp. After his arrest by the Soviet authorities, in 1939 he would presumably have been one of those who had smoother hands, at the hand inspection point that Marian spoke of, which might have determined his future. He was a lot older than Marian, aged 43 when he was initially detained by the Red Army at Chmielek and was then 'sent to a prison camp in a former cloister in Starobilsk' near Kharkov[12] along with 4,000 other officers.[ix] Czapski was moved in April 1940 to the Griazovets camp with a few of the other prisoners from Starobilsk. Czapski was one of 395 officers who were spared execution and unlike 22,000 Polish military personnel who were secretly massacred and hidden in mass burial pits.

The officers who were detained at Griazovets, were some of Poland's most highly educated military personnel, and while they were held at the prison camp they were subjected to many hours of interrogation. These men were potentially more useful to the NKVD alive. They had been moved from the prison camps at Starobilsk, Kozelsk and Ostashkov, where all of the arrested Polish officers were kept as prisoners of war and every one of them should have been protected under the terms of the Geneva Convention.

Whilst the officers, including Czapski, were detained at Griazovets they educated one another using their intellect and talents, and a nickname for the prison camp evolved, 'The Griazovets University'. These men had absolutely no idea that their friends and compatriots

---

12 Kharkov is now called Kharkiv and is in Ukraine.

had been transported and exterminated, they assumed that they were just being held in different prison camps. Czapski however, and a selected group of Polish officers, were spared execution but *'were keenly aware that their captors might kill them'*.[x]

In his book *Lost Time* published in French in 1987, Czapski describes his conditions in captivity, with temperatures being below -45°C, sleeping in lice-ridden beds, and being fed on thin soup and bad potatoes, which caused more illness than nourishment. Czapski was born in 1896, so he was 26 years older than Marian and had been conscripted into the Polish Army in 1939, as an officer. The outbreak of war impacted everyone living in Poland, the wealthy, the poor, the educated and the privileged. Czapski had an aristocratic background, and had lived in France, studying literature, art and music mixing with distinguished musicians such as Gabriel Fauré and Franz Liszt. He became an admirer of the novelist Marcel Proust. He was born in Prague in Czechoslovakia, and grew up in Minsk, before studying at university in St Petersburg, moving to the Academy of Fine Arts in Warsaw, Poland. He was originally a pacifist but volunteered for the Polish Army and was awarded the 'Virtuti Militari'[13] for his bravery on an armoured train on the fronts during the Polish–Soviet War 1918–1921. Despite a very different upbringing to Marian, Czapski's military prowess was recognised but it is important to remember that the bravery and courage of thousands of soldiers like Marian should also be commended.

The overworked, starving inmates of Griazovets actively resisted continued efforts by the NKVD to *'convert them to the Bolshevik cause'* but made efforts to boost their morale by talking to one another about their pre-war lives.[xi] As Czapski had studied the novels written by Marcel Proust, he chose this as a subject to share with the other officers. The lectures that he gave to the other prisoners, before they attempted to sleep in their freezing prison, were given based purely on memory, as Proust's books were not

---

13 Virtuti Militari – Poland's highest military decoration for heroism and courage in war.

A Polish Voice

available to him. Notes that he made relating to these lectures survived and were published in French as *'Proust W Griazowcu'* (Proust at Griazovets) in 1987. The works were later translated into English by Eric Karpeles and published again as *Lost Time*. The book demonstrates how Czapski's original lectures became a form of distraction, absorbing the officers in deep thought, giving them hope of survival when they were acutely aware of the fragility of their mortality, by showing them there was other topics to think about than their captivity:[14] *'Czapski's talks introduced a breath of humanity into an inhuman environment.'*[xii]

Marian's train journey continued northward during the latter part of 1939 taking him and other captured Polish soldiers to the White Sea on the north-west coast of Russia. In early autumn until late spring the sea there gets cold enough to freeze, but the ice is not stationary due to strong currents and tides. Marian remembered the sea being frozen. He would have arrived at Arkhangelsk.

Moscow to White Sea Map

---

14 Czapski's life was spared, unlike most of the inmates of Starobilsk, during the spring of 1940, who were shot by the NKVD and buried in mass graves in a forest at Piatykhatky, close to Kharkiv, Ukraine. He lived to the age of 96 and his witness accounts of World War Two imprisonment contributed to another book *'Inhuman Land'* which he wrote when he reached safety in Iran in 1942.

A Polish Voice

Moscow to Arkhangelsk by train is about 760 miles. Arkhangelsk was Russia's first international commercial seaport before the foundation of St Petersburg in 1703. This city, the second largest in Russia became known both as Petrograd and Leningrad during the 20th century but reverted to St Petersburg in 1991. Thousands of prisoners had taken this same journey before Marian, when Stalin initiated his 'five-year plan'. During 1929–1933 forced labour camps in Arkhangelsk, were set up to manage the forestry industry. Prisoners coped with dreadful food shortages and the living conditions were appalling. The first Soviet gulag camp was built on the Solovetsky Islands, located in the White Sea, on the site of a former Russian Orthodox monastery. The monks who had previously lived there were expelled and ordered into forced labour. The camp became responsible for labour provision needed for the construction of the Belomorkanal which opened on 2 August 1933. The Belomorkanal is the Russian name for the canal, which is a vital link for trade as it connects to Lake Onega, giving access to the Baltic Sea. It was constructed mostly by hand, by thousands of convicts, who had to dig through solid rock to build large wooden locks, so that canal boats carrying cargo could make the inland journey. The canal is still in use, but the depth of only 4 m restricts most open sea vessels from using it. Stalin planned for it to be much deeper than it was, when it was completed, but the economic goals of his first 'five-year plan', meant that it needed to be completed within a limited timeframe.

Marian was not taken to the Solovetsky Islands as this camp was closed in 1939, before his arrival. The prisoners that were held at this camp at the time of its closure were all executed. He described being detained in hangars near the frozen White Sea, which is likely to have been a transit camp, where arrangements were made for groups of prisoners to be moved to different forced labour camps. Marian does not give enough details in the recordings to be able to establish exactly where the transit camp was located, but he was selected to be moved from here to a 'forest labour camp'.

Brian asked Marian how he had travelled from then onwards. Marian's reply was:

'travel on ski and reindeer.'

It took me quite some time to understand the word he was saying was 'reindeer', but in listening carefully and repeatedly, I established that he was describing a sleigh. This form of travel, with reindeers pulling sleighs, is commonplace in the harsh frozen landscape of the region. The prisoners were taken to a forest camp, and Marian thought he was in Siberia. He clarified that it was just before Christmas 1939 when he travelled by sleigh, but January 1940 when he arrived at the camp, so he must have had some way of knowing this. Brian asked Marian about his clothes again, and he alluded that he was still wearing his Polish Army uniform.

Meanwhile, the Polish officers who had been imprisoned at Ostashkov were aware that the Soviet Union had invaded Finland on 30 November 1939, as the camp was on the flight path of a Soviet airport. They had not, however any communication with their families, but in November 1939 the camp leaders gave them permission to write one card per month to their relatives. Many of these communications were not posted, but some got through and replies were received as the men learned that the Polish government had moved to Paris.

At Starobilsk camp the officers were given regular lice inspections and often put their underwear outside in the freezing conditions in a bid to sanitise them by freezing the parasites. Prisoners had tried to acknowledge Christmas 1939 at Ostashkov, but Polish priests held at both Kozelsk and Starobilsk were killed.

The NKVD continued to interrogate the Polish officers in order to establish the men's allegiances, and the majority were always patriotic towards Poland. When asked where they would prefer to be transferred to, after their release; Germany or the Soviet Union, some lied as they were fearful of repercussions.[15] Marian had no knowledge, as far as I am aware, of his fate in late 1939 and early 1940, but he, and all of the Polish military prisoners were resigned to their situation as POWs, unlike Polish citizens who were not protected by the Geneva Convention. Rogoyska, in her excellent book *Surviving Katyn*, wrote: '*The rules laid out in the 1929 Geneva Convention regarding the treatment of prisoners of war were familiar to the Polish Officers and informed their expectations on capture*', she also acknowledged that the wives and families of the Polish officers were moved to Kazakhstan in April 1940.[xiii] The NKVD were able to identify these people from the addresses written on the prisoners' postcards!

As the environment Marian was taken to is mostly uninhabited, I will explain a little more about the surroundings Marian would have found himself in. Most of Russia's reindeer herds live in the Taiga, a term used to describe a boreal or snow forest. It was likely then that it was somewhere within the northern Taiga area that Marian was taken to a POW camp, but as I cannot ask him, I cannot identify the exact location. The average temperature in the coldest months of the year would be between - 6°C and - 50°C. During the warmer months there is a period of about 130 days where plants grow. Due to the sun being low on the horizon for most of the year, trees with needles rather than leaves, have adapted to exist in the cold conditions and evergreen trees such as pine, spruce, larch and fir trees grow there. Broadleaf trees also survive too, including willow, birch, aspen and rowan.

When the land is not snow-covered, grasses, moss, lichens, morels, mushrooms and different types of berries grow, all providing a food source for the animals that live in the Taiga. Animals that hibernate, such as bears, and marmots will stock up on berries during the summer months, eating blueberries, bilberries and wild currants. The protein-

---

15 Polish officers, who remained alive, held at Griazovets in 1941, spent a second Christmas in this prison and but still tried to acknowledge the festival by holding a secret mass. There was some music permitted by the Soviet guards, 'so long as there were no demonstrations of patriotic or religious feelings'. [Rogoyska 2021: 126: 2021]

rich mushrooms provide reindeer with nutrients, needed for the natural but aggressive process of rutting, where the males fight each other with their antlers in order to compete for the attention of the female cows. This annual sexual male reindeer activity awakens the females' hormones so that mating can take place, and results in a herd's calves being born at about the same time every year.

Reindeers can run at great speed for many hours so Marian could have travelled a large distance into the Taiga. He remembered arriving at the camp and was given orders to build his own shelter. This would have been routine in the northern logging labour camps. One of the camps that fits this description was Kotlas located in the region of Arkhangelsk Oblast which did not require guards as its location in the Taiga meant that escape was virtually impossible, due the low temperatures.

Marian did not speak of anyone else being detained there other than soldiers, but as there was a network of camps at Kotlas, there may have been segregation. His captors, he explained, were older Russian men. He gave a clear description of the sleeping arrangements in the accommodation that he and the other prisoners had to build themselves. Their bunks were constructed from wooden planks with two men sleeping on the top and

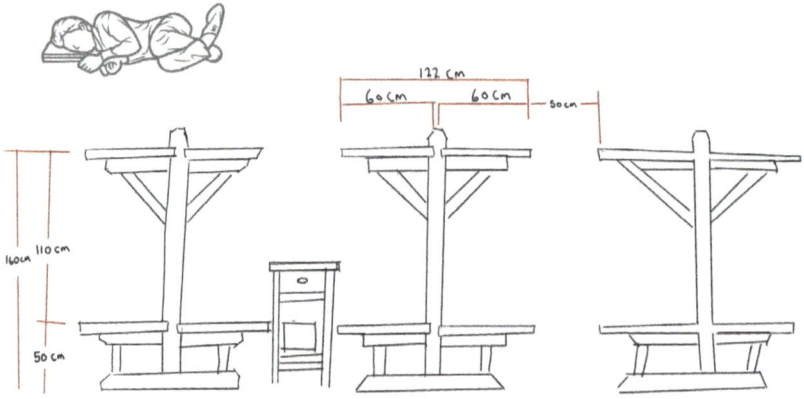

This image shows six wooden sleeping bunks used in GULAG labour camps. The sketch is based on a drawing by Jacques Rossi in The Gulag Handbook.

three on the bottom. The cabin was surrounded with 10 ft of snow and inside there was probably one small fire. The prisoners would have slept in their clothes but may have had reindeer hides to use as blankets. Marian was instructed to cut a particular type of tree for the bunks which needed to be trimmed to a certain size, then he had to clean the wood and save only the good quality material. Larch trees were used quite a bit for this purpose.

Marian spoke about how many prisoners died from starvation while they were kept at the camp, as there was very little food available to them. The Soviet Union's NKVD kept thousands of people working under the communist regime in appalling, stinking, freezing conditions, where they had no other choice than to work to survive.

Another soldier who survived these conditions referred to 'the death spiral',[xiv] which began when a person who had become sick missed one day's bread ration. With a lack of food in their bodies, subsequently the sick person became weaker, so could not physically work as hard. The rations were given out based on output, so if less work was done, then a prisoner would receive a smaller quantity of bread. This was the spiral that led to many deaths, as once a person was on a downward spiral, there was no chance of recovery. The food that they did receive was very poor quality and Marian recalled that it was brought to them by Eskimos on sleighs. The food would have consisted of bread, probably black rye bread and a watery stew made from cabbage, radishes, carrots and sometimes fish heads. They also sometimes received a type of porridge made from buckwheat, a hardy grain that can thrive in poor soil conditions and has a short growing season, meaning it could be harvested between the frozen winters. Buckwheat is recorded as being an essential staple and a source of protein in ancient Russian history but would probably not have been available in the middle of the winter. Surviving on these meagre rations meant that prisoners were weak, cold and emaciated. There would have been a lot of darkness too, with only a few hours of light at that time of year reaching northern hemisphere.

In Kozelsk some food and clothing parcels did get through to the officers, sent from families who had received cards, but the majority did not. They must have been experiencing better living conditions than Marian was. The address the relatives were given for posting the parcels to the officers was 'the Maxim Gorky Rest Home'[xv] as the NKVD did not want to give away the location of their prison camp.

Brian asked Marian if there was much brutality from the Russian soldiers, but he said not, and that they were just left to get on with the work. With repetitive strenuous daily effort and small amounts of food, just staying alive was his biggest challenge. It was said that 'Men would have given a handful of diamonds for an extra slice of bread'[xvi]

These were Marian's words from the tape:

'lots of dying, lots of men dying as no food, hard work and cold, and lots of bloomin' fleas, lice, lice everywhere'.

Lice were rife in prison camps, and he may also have been referring to mosquitoes, that hatch in the summer months, after attaching themselves to reindeers' coats during the winter. They would be embedded into animal skins which were undoubtedly used by prisoners for warmth, and the mosquitoes' natural cycle of being dormant in the winter months may have been disturbed, by a little warmth inside the prison shelters. Human lice multiply in overcrowded conditions and are the cause of infection and disease spreading quickly, particularly typhus. Prisoners would have been contaminated as poor hygiene was inevitable, which Marian confirmed when he said that people were dying of the flies.

One of the other Polish prisoners at the camp was a higher-ranking army major, who had obviously passed the previous 'hand check test', and seemed to be a big influence on Marian, as it was he, according to Marian's account on the tape, who suggested that he should plan an escape. The major might well have recognised the young man's determined character and tried to help his comrade, or I suspect, that it may have been easier for Marian to tell Brian that he had innocently obtained some of the major's belongings. Marian said that the major had concealed a compass and a gold watch and when he became ill and realised that he would not survive, he donated his valuable belongings to Marian. He also said that the major, knowing that he would perish himself, gave Marian instructions that when he died, which he knew he would, Marian was to remove the clothes from his body and wear them himself. So, either the major was a selfless soldier, who knew he was about to die, or Marian preferred to not tell Brian that he had stolen the valuables from a dying man, to help with his escape. We will never know, but understandably the survival instinct would have been the dominant influence on Marian at this time.

With typhus infecting soldiers at the camp, there was some attempt from the Soviet Soldiers to provide medical attention, but it did not sound as though there was any form of medicine being issued as Marian mentioned that a doctor did attend him, but that he had just given him a sip of vodka. He very much feared that he was going to become ill too.

Marian mentioned that he saved his food up for several days, despite feeling desperately hungry as he knew that he would need sustenance if he left the camp. In his recorded account he revealed that he and three other Polish soldiers left the forest prison camp during the night, without anyone preventing them from doing so. Marian said they passed Eskimos, who he believed hated the Russian soldiers, so he knew that they would not have stopped them. Marian could only remember one of the men's names that he escaped with, Yanick, who was younger than himself. The other two soldiers, he said were both older than him.

Marian spoke quite a bit about the Eskimos who helped him and his comrades after their escape. He was referring to indigenous ethnic minorities who live in the northern parts of the Soviet Union and Siberia. There are several native groups. The Eveny people live in the north-east, and exist by living closely with reindeer herds, moving about with them as they migrate. The Evenki people also live in Siberia and both of these nomadic people use the Tungusic language. Wild reindeer roam in Siberia as well as farmed herded animals, with several different species existing there, some being more suitable for domestication, for riding and tolerating wearing a harness so that they can pull sleighs. Without the help Marian received from the indigenous people, he would probably not have survived. He mentioned them quite a bit on the tapes and explained how they gave him food and taught him how to survive in the freezing conditions. The Eveny people's lives are extremely intertwined with the reindeer that they live with, they use their skin as clothing, drink their milk, eat their meat and trade their antlers which is an important ingredient in Korean and Chinese medicines, so can have a high value for trading. The Eveny people practice Shamanism, a religious spirituality which connects human and animal life.

When Stalin was operating his collectivisation plan in the 1930s, the reindeer herds became state owned, but the herding was still operational as humans needed to follow the migration of the herds in order to survive. Although some of the reindeer become domesticated, the movement of the large herds is perpetual and reindeer herding is commonplace in Siberia to this day.

Marian's plan to escape, he claimed, was not made alone, telling Brian that it involved the three other men, who all left the camp together. They had learnt how to make special snowshoes from willow tree wood. A snowshoe allows a person to distribute their body weight over a larger area, making it less likely for them to sink into the snow. Willow would be flexible enough to bend into shape to form the type of shoe that was needed, and it does grow in the Taiga. Traditional Siberian snowshoes would have also been made from reindeer hide.

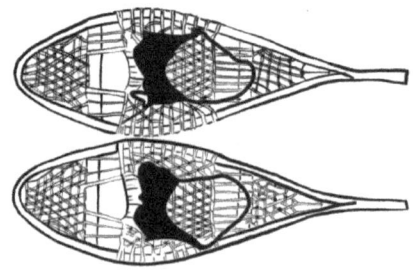

Traditional snowshoe

Marian's voice became very weak and feeble in some of the tape recordings, and I think that the dreadful events he was attempting to recall were a contributory factor. He told Brian the circumstances of the death of one of his comrades. Marian recounted how the escapees had been trying to cross a frozen river when one man fell through a gap in the ice. Marian recalled the horror of seeing the soldier's eyes looking up at him, from below the ice, a stark reminder of how dangerous their escape plan was and said that he had nearly fallen over himself, but his heightened self-survival instinct always put his own safety first and he made no attempts to rescue the other man. Sharing the details of this incident with Brian in the hospital years later, caused him great anguish as the emotion in his voice can be clearly heard. It was these intimate details, and the fervour in Marian's voice that made listening to his story compulsive to me.

The weather and survival conditions were so bleak Marian said that it claimed the lives of both the two older soldiers leaving only Marian and Yanick alone in the freezing conditions. He did not give any more information though about the death of the second older soldier.

Marian did spend some time explaining to Brian about the type of boots he had worn in addition to the snowshoes that he had made when he left the forest prison camp. He described them as being made of a special material and explained how he created a suit of armour, on the outside of the boots, using ice. This practice, I have discovered can be very effective. Marian, I assume was wearing his Polish Army issued boots, but got the idea of protecting them in this way, from the Eskimos. The native Eskimos were likely to have worn woollen, felted, Valenki type boots. Marian talked about a special material that was inside his boots, which was probably wool. Traditional Russian Valenki boots are made by squashing many layers of wool and then shrinking the boot to fit onto the foot. These types of boots are not waterproof, but they don't need to be when used for walking on soft snow. They can be worn with a rubber outer layer. It is probable that this type of boot would have been issued to Marian's captors, the Soviet soldiers, so Marian may have stolen them.

Marian understood that he and his comrade needed to head towards the Ural Mountains.[16] He said this was because there were not many Soviet soldiers there, only the friendly Eskimo inhabitants. I don't know how he gained this information, but as the majority of his knowledge appears to have come from the Eskimo people, they must have taught him survival techniques. Without their support and guidance, it is doubtful Marian would have survived.

Brian asked Marian if he could speak Russian and he said that as it was similar to Polish, he was able to pick it up very quickly, but I think this just highlights Marian's adaptability and intelligence, and his tenacity and determination to survive.

Marian with his single companion Yanick, were directed to a lake by the Eskimo people which Marian described as being warm with steam rising from the water. I think he was describing a hot spring. He said that he saw lots of fish and eagle and a bear and that he and Yanick stayed there for several days and were able to rest. He mentioned seeing the moon, but not the sun, which he said he never saw, only dark cloud in the daylight hours. He also referred to a special pair of stones (flint) that the Eskimos gave them, that enabled them to light a fire. In his own words from the tape Marian said:

'Special stones, Eskimos give it and you make it, this material burning … you know … and you blow up and you make a fire … and keep it … animals, bear out … we pick salmon out … water not very deep, lovely warm, steam coming out. One night I caught lots of salmon and in the night, I eat it all'.

---

16 The Ural Mountain range runs north to south through Russia into Kazakhstan. A train runs between the Ural Mountains to the Caspian Sea.

Brian replied: *'You never ate its head?'*

'Only the best bits,'

replied Marian, and he laughed saying:

'yes the best bits!'

The humorous exchanges between the two men on the tape recording, shows how well they were getting on together in Bournemouth Hospital, and I wonder if sharing with Brian the events that Marian had experienced many years earlier was quite therapeutic for the pair of them.

I have wondered what the hospital staff must have thought of Brian recording and interviewing Marian in his hospital bed. There was no secrecy in what they were doing so the staff must have been comfortable with it. Perhaps it was beneficial to both of their recoveries and provided a distraction from feeling unwell. Sometimes other noises from the ward can be heard on the tape, such as the floors being cleaned in the background.

Marian's voice recording becomes feeble and perhaps a bit emotional again when he tells Brian what happened to his friend Yanick. As the two men continue their journey, Marian's comrade becomes very unwell. Marian's voice gradually gets weaker and quieter as he shares the details of his friend's death. The tape recording was both difficult and compulsive listening for me. He explained that it was too cold for them to sleep and how the Eskimos had showed them how to get some rest by digging a shelter in the snow but insisted that they should not remain in the hole for more than one or two hours otherwise they would freeze to death. In Marian's own words he said:

> 'All weeks, all nights we walked and he not very well, Yanick. I said well don't be silly come on! We dig a hole and go to sleep. All gone, never saw nothing else. I wake in the morning, he is gone. Thought he gone toilet, but his body laid out stiff.'

Brian repeated Marian's words slowly, and when he realised that his friend had just recounted the awful moment that his last travelling companion had died. Brian offered him compassionate listening skills, something he was very good at throughout his life, and he was giving Marian the chance to talk about the death of his friend, which he may never have spoken about to anyone before. Marian sadly recounted that his companion's body was laid out stiff and frozen. On the tape there is a brief pause before Brian encouraged him to tell him what happened next. He gently asked Marian if he had taken Yanick's clothes, as he had heard how Marian had taken the clothes belonging to the Major, back at the prison camp. Marian told him that he didn't take them, that he had left his friend clothed, but remembered how he had motivated himself by saying to himself:

> 'Marian, you only left, I say well you must pull your socks, you by yourself'.

No one will ever know who Yanick was. Thousands of young Polish soldiers' lives ended tragically in the freezing territories of the Soviet Union. I am just grateful to be able to write about one who did survive.

Marian kept walking on alone and he was clearly grateful for the food, encouragement and directions the Eskimos had given him on his lonely walk. They gave him dried reindeer to eat. He described it being chewy like gum. He told Brian that he was still walking in deep snow, but his recall of events, became quite muddled at times, as he sounded tired and unwell in this part of the tape recordings.

Eventually, Marian found his way to a railway station, that was on the Trans-Siberian Railway line, which runs between Mongolia and Siberia.[17] He remembered that he had travelled aboard a train for about a week, but does not describe the journey, however, he did confess that at one particular railway station he stole a woman's suitcase. This does give a bit more credibility to my theory that he may well have stolen the Major's possessions back at the forest prison camp. When Brian asked him why he had done that, Marian told him that it was for food, explaining that cloth was worth a bit of money. His criminality was obviously linked with severe hunger and survival. Marian described boarding a goods train that was carrying food supplies. He said that he thought this was useful as there was plenty to eat on the train but the marrows and grapes that he stole gave him diarrhoea. Marian's tone of voice indicated that this was not a good memory but spoke of how he had been advised by someone to eat cotton, which would alleviate the symptoms of an upset stomach. He said that he had never eaten a marrow or a grape since that time! Cotton leaf tea is meant to have therapeutic health benefits, and is sometimes used as a herbal treatment for respiratory diseases and inflammation, so I am not convinced that Marian received the correct advice.

One of Marian's good and memorable meals was a chicken. He recounted how he had stolen one and cooked it in clay. He said that he was picking cotton seed, he worked doing this presumably in order to obtain enough money to buy a train ticket. He said that he saw a chicken and stole it and put it in a clay pot. Marian's exact words were:

'chicken cook after night gone, fetched it and I have meat, lovely chicken taste'.

---

17 The Trans-Siberian railway runs along the Urals. The station at Yekaterinburg is 1,126 miles to the Caspian Sea.

Marian's repetitive and extraordinary resourcefulness gives me a lot of pleasure to write about in this unusual memoir, and his incredible story of escape from the forest prison camp is a one that deserves respect, but I have found it frustrating not to be able to validate his exact route. There are aspects of the journey that he described to my dad that don't completely make sense to me geographically, but he is no longer here to ask, so I have recorded the details as well as I can. However, in Chapter 3, you will learn how Marian's life adventure is only just beginning at this point, and many of the events he spoke of in the recordings I have been able to compare with facts, so effectively prove Marian's story to be true.

In the next chapter we leave the Soviet Union and head south across the Caspian Sea. Marian survived captivity in the Soviet Union, but thousands of people continued to suffer imprisonment in forced labour and gulag-style camps for many more years. How much Marian knew about the extensive horrors that continued in the Soviet Union at the time will never be known, as his focus was just to reach a place of safety. Gulag camps continued to operate under the administration of the NKVD up until 1953 with more than 18 million people having been recorded as living in them at some point. They existed until the end of the Soviet Union in 1991.

CHAPTER 3

Marian's escape from the Soviet forest prison camp is incredible in itself but in this chapter, I will explain how his recorded voice revealed enough information for me to be able to discover how he managed to become reunited with the Polish Army.

Alone after the death of his comrade Yanick, still using his estimable initiative, Marian, we know worked for a while picking cotton, which allowed him to earn some money. He said he earned 20 roubles, which was enough to buy a train ticket. This ticket enabled him to board a goods train that took him to a port on the Caspian Sea. Marian described it as an 'oldish town' in Kazakhstan. This would have been the port of Atyrau, located at the north of the Ural River, as a freight train line ran directly to this port. Brian asked him if anyone had asked for his papers while he was travelling on the train, but he told him that if anyone asked, he just told them that he had lost them.

The Caspian Sea is the biggest inland body of water in the world, at 143 square miles, its minimum width across measures 124 miles, increasing to 270 miles at the widest point. It has coastlines with five countries, Russia, Kazakhstan, Turkmenistan, Azerbaijan and Iran, its classic Greek and Persian name was the Hyrcanian Ocean. Arguments over it being a categorised as a sea or a lake, are due to its water salinity being less than a third of other world oceans. More than 130 rivers flow into it with the biggest being the Volga and the second the Ural. In addition to having a mineral rich seabed, in oil and gas, the fish that live in the water include six species of sturgeon. These are the type of fish that produce the food delicacy caviar. One of those six is the famed Beluga Sturgeon which sells for the highest price. A summit held in the port city, Aktau[18] in Kazakhstan during August 2018 settled an agreement over this long-standing argument of its status as a sea or a lake. It was decided, by the delegates visiting this city, which has no street names, that the sea would be given a special status, with the surface remaining a common area, but the seabed would be divided up between each of the five surrounding countries. Fishing boundaries were also agreed.

Atyrau originated as a fishing settlement in the 17th century. Fishing and associated trade were the main economic activities of the port, until a large oil refinery was commissioned there. When Marian arrived there by train in 1940 it was purely a fishing port. He watched the boats that were being loaded with fish and learned that the catch was to be shipped to Iran (described by Marian as Persia). He decided that he should try to become a hideaway on board one of these fishing boats.

He sounded as though he enjoyed telling Brian how he hid himself in a wooden fishing barrel aboard one of the boats. Somehow, he managed to conceal himself for about eight hours, for the duration of the sea crossing. Brian asked him about the temperature as he wondered if the fish were being kept chilled, but Marian reassured him that it was quite warm compared to where he had been in the forest labour camp. The two of them sounded quite amused at this, knowing that the conditions were far more favourable for Marian than they had been a few months previously.

The fishing boat would have arrived in one of the many ports on the Iranian coast. Marian always referred to this part of the world as Persia, but this country was called Iran from 1935. He was undoubtedly damp and smelly having travelled in a fish barrel and mentioned that he needed to get some clean and presentable clothes. On the tape recordings Marian explained to Brian how he went to a shopping area during the night and broke into a very old shop where he stole clothes,

---

18 Aktau has no street names, as it was founded as a work camp by Stalin and became one of the Soviet Union's closed cities. It is arranged in numbered districts. An address might look like this: 9-12-42, with the first number being the district, the second the building and the third the apartment or business.

before looking for somewhere to sleep. Another disclosure of theft!

It is difficult to know how much information Marian would have had access to about the progress of the war, and what he knew about the plight of other Polish servicemen at the time. His determination to survive each unique situation though always showed initiative and ingenuity in resolving them.

In one of the recorded sound bites Marian spoke about a fig tree that was growing on the outskirts of a village that he passed, whilst he was walking inland in Iran, which he said gave him the opportunity to have something to eat. He recounted how these figs had the same effect on his digestive system as the grapes and the marrow had done when he was aboard the goods train. Marian said to Brian:

'oh no, fig, never eat any more after that'!

Marian seemed aware that he needed to be as well-groomed as possible, and he said that he tried to keep himself clean by washing in rivers and streams. He recounted an encounter with two strangers, two men who offered to help him. It was quite difficult for me to understand what Marian was saying on the tape recording, as it sounded as though he was suffering from hiccups in the hospital! I think he was trying to explain to Brian that he wanted to get to the capital of Iran. The two men gave Marian a train ticket to Tehran, which is about 95 miles inland from the coast, When Brian quizzed Marian as to who these men were, he said that he thought that they were probably British soldiers. Marian's exact words on the tape:

'I told them who I am, well after I told them … well, we British'.

I can only assume that these men must have been British soldiers who were arranging for Marian to be taken into British custody, as Iran was under British rule at this time.

A Polish Voice

The two men, who had given Marian a train ticket, travelled on the same train as him and on their arrival in Tehran, they took him to a hotel. The two strangers could speak Russian and Polish, and I think it is likely, from what Marian said that they were trying to establish his nationality. When they had satisfied themselves that he was in fact Polish, he was sent to Tobruk in Libya, where other surviving Polish soldiers were being sent and he was told, that as a Polish soldier, he would be ordered to rejoin Polish troops in Britain.

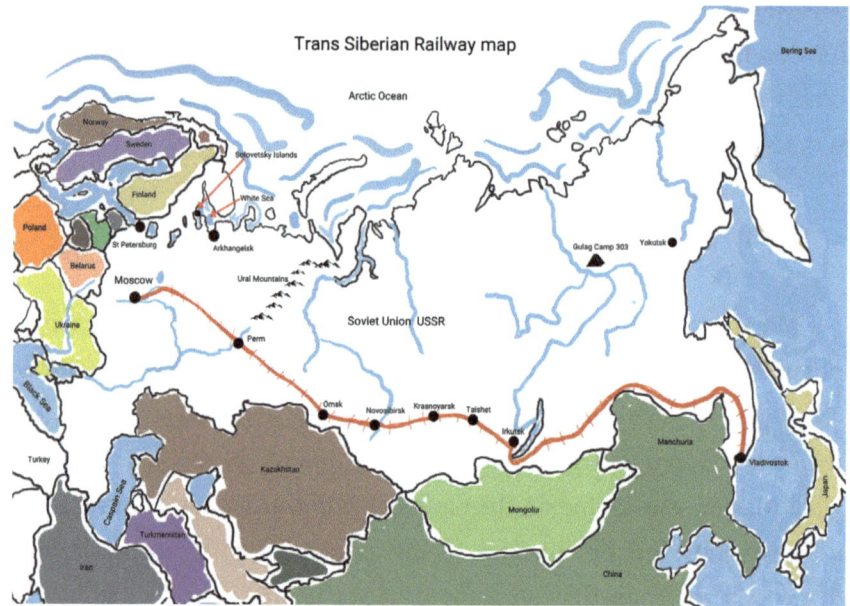

Map of Trans-Siberian Railway

Marian was then sent to Alexandria in Egypt, where he joined the Royal Mail Ship Mauretania at the Suez Canal. He remembered crowds of people including children being packed onto the ship that sailed for the United Kingdom via Durban in South Africa, around Cape Horn.

RMS Mauretania sailed to Scotland where Marian became reunited with other Polish troops who were stationed there. Scotland received a huge influx of soldiers from Poland, with most arriving after the German occupation of France in June 1940. Depending on how long it had taken for Marian to travel back by ship, it was likely that these events coincided, so he must have felt extremely pleased to see so many of his compatriots.

Scotland was not very well protected against German attacks at this time, so the Polish military forces were welcomed. The Polish Army units were subordinate to the British Army, but their contribution to operations were important. The Polish military patrolled the Scottish coastline, whilst building their own camps and infrastructure, and were controlled from headquarters that were based at Eastend House near Thankerton in Lanarkshire.

'The Fall of France' or the 'Surrender of France', as it became known, had an impact on Brian's family living in the south of England. On 5 June 1940, one day before his 6th birthday, German forces initiated '*Fall Rot*' (Case Red), a military operation that led to a signed armistice between Germany and France, with around 1.8 million French soldiers becoming prisoners of war and French civilians facing a future of Nazi German occupation.

A French Army officer, Fernard Le Bret, was one of 340,000 allied troops evacuated from the Dunkirk beaches. He was taken aboard a crowded British warship which was under fire from German planes and arrived in Folkestone in Kent. Le Bret and another officer were sent to Weymouth where they were to be billeted. Brian had two aunts, Beatrice Wilkins (who liked to be known as May) and her sister Winifred. They went along to the billeting administration which was held at the Weymouth Grammar School. The two young ladies invited these two soldiers to their parents; Emily and Sidney's house in New Close Gardens, where they stayed for several weeks. Le Bret and the other officer returned to Cherbourg in France later in the year on a merchant ship and they managed to make their way on stolen bicycles to the South of France where they found safety.

It was at around the same time during 1940, that Marian rejoined the Polish Army in Scotland, but this time there was brief as he was sent back into military operations in Tobruk, Libya within a month. It is quite difficult to imagine how he must have felt about this after he had travelled so many miles around the world. Marian's voice was upbeat, when he spoke about his duty as a soldier though, and said:

'no good complaining'.

He told Brian how he was reunited with comrades and Brian was interested in how they had escaped. Marian thought that 36 soldiers from Warsaw had managed to get to Africa. Many Polish servicemen escaped from Poland across the borders of Romania, Hungary and Czechoslovakia, to join the forces who gathered in France, whilst others had been captured by the Soviet Union's NKVD and were sent to Northern Russia and Siberia. Marian, now serving as a Polish soldier again, together with a Gurkha regiment was sent to Tobruk in Libya to relieve British soldiers who were stationed there.

At this same time, Brian, then six years old, after his birthday in June 1940, was registered as a pupil at Holy Trinity Infant School in Weymouth, Dorset. He walked to school with his friend Billy Monger from his home in Clearmount Road, Rodwell, where he lived with his mother and father. His mother Ida would have had her daughter Rosemary, born in March, to care for at home, and his father worked full time at the torpedo factory at Bincleaves, so setting off to school on their own was something these young boys did regularly. On the morning of 4 July however, they experienced a sight that would remain with them for the rest of their lives.

Portland Harbour was an important Naval base during World War Two. Her Majesty's Ship Foylebank[19] was anchored in Portland Harbour, following a reconnaissance mission, the previous day, the ship

---

[19] HMS Foylebank was a merchant vessel that had been requisitioned in 1939, was converted into an anti-aircraft ship and had proven effective in combat against the German Luftwaffe.

was considered to be an important target for the German Luftwaffe. The ship flew a yellow flag when enemy planes were expected and a red flag when planes were reported to be approaching Portland. Due to confusion over unidentified aircraft that were thought to be allied air forces returning to base, the yellow flag was flying at breakfast time just as Brian and his friend were on their way to school. Out of the clear blue, sunny morning sky, 26 German Stuka planes attacked HMS Foylebank for a period of eight minutes. In a later interview with Brian in 2019 these were his exact memories:

'When I was six, one day, we were going to school with my friend Billy Monger, and we just got to Rodwell railway bridge, when there was an explosion in Portland Harbour, and then we climbed up on the wall to the bridge, which you could still do now, and we watched the Stukers bombing the Foylebank.'

Brian's recollections of this event stayed with him throughout his lifetime, and later in his life he often spoke about Leading Seaman, Jack Forman Mantle, who was awarded the Victoria Cross posthumously for his bravery during the attack. Of the 298 crew, 176 were killed and many more injured. Mantle had remained at his gun position, despite receiving serious injuries, that resulted in his death. Two German Stuka bombers were shot down, but the aerial attack on the ship left it ablaze and so badly damaged, that it sank the following day.

Jack Mantle's grave

Brian would not have had the maturity to understand the impact of the event at the time, but when he met Marian in Bournemouth Hospital, he had empathy for him as he realised that both of their lives had been impacted by the war. In this same month the Home Guard was established in Britain, an armed militia, made up of local citizens who were too old or too young to join the regular army. Brian's father William took up this voluntary role in Weymouth.

Wilkins Home Guard

During 1940 around 200,000 children were evacuated from London for their safety. Brian's home life was affected by the arrival of two of these evacuees. Later, in December his school was bombed, so his education was disrupted. He was a mischievous child, and formal education never became a major part of his life. He did attend

Weymouth Grammar School, and enjoyed geography and maths, but was more interested in learning outside of the classroom. His sight was poor, and he always claimed this was due to him trying to read books under his bed covers at night with a torch, as blackout regulations were imposed in all homes and businesses after dark, to make navigation for enemy aircraft as difficult as possible.

During September 1940 the leaders of Germany, Italy and Japan signed a pact of alliance, which became known as the Axis Alliance. Securing the control of the port of Tobruk in Libya was important for British war strategy as it was a deep-water harbour that allowed for the supply of soldiers and equipment to the region. At the beginning of World War Two Tobruk was an Italian colony. It was captured from Italy by the British and Commonwealth forces in January 1941 but was continually assaulted by Axis troop offensives from Egypt. Soldiers who were stationed in Tobruk needed to be switched regularly as the fighting was relentless. In late August 1941 the Polish Independent Carpathian Brigade, made up of soldiers who were exiled after the invasion of their country, formed in French Syria, moved 5,000 of their soldiers into Tobruk, which was commanded by General Stanisław Kopański.

After three weeks of fighting in Tobruk, Marian was wounded by sniper fire in his shoulder. He said:

'bullet came out of air and out'

and he asked Brian if he would like to see the scar. Brian acknowledged that he had already seen it. Marian was keen for Brian to know that he had been helped by the Gurkha soldiers. Due to his injury the decision was made for him to return to Britain again, and using Marian's own words:

'he says you no bloomin' good here, we gonna send you back to England'.

Marian obviously found this an amusing story to tell Brian and they both laughed together at his misfortune.

The Gurkhas are regarded as some of the most respected allied troops. Their name originates from the Kingdom of Gorkha, which is now known as Nepal. During the war the Nepalese government offered Britain the full support of all its battalions as part of a field army known as the Eighth Army, which was made up of a collaboration of allied forces.

Marian, again very amused, told Brian that, due to his injury, he was once again ordered to return to the UK.

Marian was sent to Alexandria for the second time, to be evacuated, along with thousands of German prisoners of war. He boarded RMS Mauretania once again and repeated the journey that took him first to Durban in South Africa. He remembered the ship docking there and seeing children and wounded soldiers get aboard. The ship sailed onward around Cape Horn and then across the Atlantic to Canada, where he said that he understood the German prisoners of war were supposed to disembark, but Marian who sounded quite amused, stated:

'we don't want blooming Jerrys'.

He was referring to the Canadian's refusal to take the prisoners at this time. He remembered then, how the ship had sailed to America, but the American authorities didn't permit the prisoners ashore either, so RMS Mauretania returned to Paisley in Scotland. Some of the passengers aboard, however, had become ill with typhus, so they were not permitted to disembark in Paisley for about three weeks. Marian thought that there were other Polish soldiers aboard RMS Mauretania, that had been wounded fighting in Tobruk, like himself.

The RMS Mauretania, that Marian travelled aboard twice, was the second ship to be given that name. The first was retired in 1935, and in order to safeguard her name while the new ship was being built, the owners, Cunard White Star, asked a Southampton company, Red

Funnel Steamers, if they would rename one of their paddle steamers Mauretania until the new ship was finished. They agreed and a paddle steamer called Queen, that was used for excursions on the south coast, took the name until the new ship was launched.

On 28 July 1938, a very windy day in Merseyside, Lady Bates, wife of Sir Percy Pates the chairman of Cunard White Star Shipping Line, stood on an open-air platform built especially for the launch ceremony. With a strong north-west wind blowing her clothes and hair, she announced:

This is a red-letter day, not only for me but for Merseyside. The launch of the largest ship that has ever been built in England. I hope that like her namesake she may work her way into the affections of all who have to do with her on both sides of the Atlantic. To the ship and all who serve or sail in her I wish all good fortune. I name you Mauretania.

Then with one hand on her hat, she vigorously swung a bottle of champagne with the other against the dark hull of the ship. A huge crowd of 40,000 cheered as Lady Bates then wound a small winch handle drawing back British and American flags, that had been concealing the brass lettering that spelled the ship's name. The ship then slowly glided backwards into the River Mersey as a band struck up the patriotic anthem 'Rule Britannia'. Nine tugs were on hand to guide the rudderless RMS Mauretania into a wet basin, where 3,000 workmen continued to fit her out. In order to fit her 50-ton rudder she was moved from the wet basin to Gladstone Graving Dock, before her speed trials began in the Firth of Clyde. Percy Bates pleased with her performance accepted her with pride into the Cunard White Star fleet.

The ship did not leave Birkenhead docks until nearly a year later when she sailed on her maiden voyage to New York on 17 June 1939. When she arrived back on 6 August to King George V Dock in London, again thousands turned out to see her. She left on her second paid passenger cruise but returned from New York with fewer passengers than were originally booked due to the political tensions that were increasing in Europe. When Germany invaded Poland on 1

September 1939, RMS Mauretania was in the middle of the Atlantic and on her arrival back to Southampton, she was requisitioned by the British government. Only 14 months after being launched, this cruise ship, which had been painted in smart Cunard White Star colours was quickly painted battleship grey and fitted with armoury and guns. She went back to New York during September and again in December 1939, with a small number of passengers, but mostly cargo. In March 1940 RMS Mauretania was instructed to serve as a troopship so departed New York, bound for Sydney, Australia, where her luxury interior was transformed and fitted with bunks, hammocks and mess tables, giving her the capacity to carry 6,500 troops. Her first mission as a troop ship was part of a convoy that left Sydney on 5 May 1940, sailing towards the Firth of Clyde in Scotland. After this she continued to sail on the route that became known as the 'Suez Shuffle', calling at Bombay, Colombo, Durban and the Egyptian Port Tawfiq[20] near Port Said and Alexandria, until 1943. A route that Marian became very familiar with!

During World War Two, RMS Mauretania travelled 540,000 miles and transported over 350,000 troops. After the war ended, she continued to be used in government service, repatriating troops and civilians, and during 1946 Mauretania was used to carry war brides and their children, including 364 babies, to Canada. Once released from government service she undertook a complete refurbishment and the workforce at Cammell Laird's shipbuilding yard in Birkenhead, restored her to a luxury cruise ship once more. RMS Mauretania returned to service in April 1947, with 400 honoured guests aboard for a two-night shakedown cruise to the Hebrides, but gale force winds meant that the captain had to seek shelter in a bay on the north-east of Anglesey. He anchored, but the anchor dragged on the seabed, so the ship was tossing about in the Irish Sea until the winds abated. Undoubtedly a memorable cruise for many! From then on until 1957 she made 260 Atlantic crossings as a

---

20 Port Tawfiq – the Suez Canal entrance.

luxury cruise liner once again. Mauretania underwent another refit in Southampton in 1957, when air conditioning was fitted and in 1962, she was painted a pale green colour. With a declining number of people booking to travel on this ship the amount of staff became larger than the number of passengers, making the cost of keeping her running too high, so it was decided that she be withdrawn from service.

RMS Mauretania took her last voyage in 1965 before she was completely scrapped in 1966. The ship's bell is installed at the Williamson Art Gallery and Museum in Birkenhead, Merseyside. Lord and Lady Bates' only son, who was also named Percy like his father, was killed on New Year's Day 1945, whilst serving as a pilot in the RAF in a mission flying over Germany.

Having arrived back in Paisley for a second time in 1941, presumably after receiving medical attention for his wounded shoulder, Marian was likely to have travelled by train to a transit camp in Scotland and subsequently would have become a member of the 1st (Polish) Independent Parachute Brigade[21] who were under the command of Major General Stanislaw Sosabowski. This brigade was formed in Leven in Scotland on 23 September and incorporated soldiers who had escaped in circumstances similar to Marian's, and others who had escaped Nazi held Poland, via France. The headquarters were at Largo house, a stately home, which was requisitioned by the army. A parachute tower was built near there, which allowed troops to practise jumping. Allied troops also trained here, including the Free French Forces. Each paratrooper, as part of their training, also had to attend a four-week course at RAF Ringway in Cheshire. On the tape, Marian spoke to Brian about being sent to Ringway. Brian asked him how his language was at this point, and he said that he was beginning to pick up

---

21 The 1st (Polish) Independent Parachute Brigade was formed by the Polish government, who were exiled in London in 1941 while the exiled Prime Minister of Poland was also trying to give strategic support to the Polish resistance movement 'Armia Krajowa' which was later formed in 1942 in Poland.

more English. He remembered that he was in a group with one other Polish soldier and two English ones. The Polish Brigade wore British uniforms, including rimless parachute helmets. The Polish insignia of an eagle was stencilled onto these, and when these were not being worn, a grey beret distinguished them from the 1st British Airborne troops who wore maroon ones.

RAF Station Ringway is now Manchester Airport. A public terminal opened in 1938 and the RAF station opened in June 1940 and became the main parachute training school during World War Two. Here, 60,000 paratroopers from all allied forces were trained, along with the development of military gliders.[22]

The 1st Polish Parachute Brigade gradually grew in strength, as more Polish soldiers that had been POWs reached Britain. During this same summer a pact was signed on 30 July 1941 between the Soviet Ambassador and General Sikorski, in London. This was called the Sikorski–Mayski agreement, its purpose was to re-establish Polish Soviet relations after Germany had invaded the Soviet Union. A division of the Polish Army within the Soviet Union was agreed. Some Polish officers were pleased about this, but many others were not as they wanted to rejoin the exiled Polish Army in Britain. This led to divisions between the opinions of some of the Polish Generals who has been incarcerated in the Soviet Union. One of these officers was General Władysław Anders, who had been imprisoned and tortured in Lubyanka Prison in Moscow but had always resisted the NKVD's pressure to persuade him to join the Red Army. He was released on 4 August 1941 and General Sikorski appointed him to lead a Polish division, while both men continued to try to establish what had happened to thousands of their missing comrades who had been held at the three prison camps, at Ostashkov, Kozelsk and Starobilsk, in 1940. Both Polish Generals met with Stalin on 3 December 1941 in Moscow, and they complained to

---

22 The Airborne Delivery Wing is now based at RAF Brize Norton.

him that some of the measures that were supposed to be achieved by the treaty they had drawn up together were not being implemented such as releasing Polish officers from prisons and camps. Stalin claimed[xvii] that all Poles had been released except for some that had run away to Manchuria.[23]

General Anders, with the support of both Churchill and Franklin D Roosevelt eventually negotiated with Stalin, that Polish troops, many ill with typhoid and malaria, should be moved out of the USSR to Iran and during early spring of 1942, the first evacuations took place. Stalin insisted that there was evidence the missing officers had been in Kolyma[24] and it was likely they had become German prisoners of war.[xviii]

He appointed Czapski as head of the Army's propaganda service, writing for the Polish Army newspapers, and he persevered with his enquiries with the NKVD about the missing men. Later, at the end of the summer, a second wave of evacuations saw thousands of starving Polish soldiers and civilians leave the Soviet Union to be transported via Krasnovodsk[25], in Turkmenistan, across the Caspian Sea to Pahlavi[26] in Iran, along with the Army, which became known as the Persian Corridor. The human suffering, and the conditions that these refugees were subjected to during transportation were atrocious. After more than two years in detention in Soviet gulags and prison camps, many were sick with typhoid and emaciated from a lack of food. The filthy smelling boats that took them across the sea, were so crammed, there was no space between human bodies on deck. Many had dysentery, and with a shortage of toilet facilities on the boat the decks became awash with human excrement. Some fell in and drowned, being too weak to hold on to the railings, when the boat pitched in the waves. There was nothing for the passengers to drink, resulting in many cases

---

23 Manchuria – part of northern China and Inner Mongolia.
24 Kolyma is within the Arctic Circle in the far east of Russia.
25 Krasnovodsk is now called Turkmenbashi.
26 Pahlavi is now called Bandar-e Anzali.

of dehydration.

When these ships docked in Pahlavi, those who had survived the transportation, were disinfected, deloused and shaved by the British Army. At a reception camp, they were given clothing and tents to sleep in. Food had to be given in small quantities as their stomachs had become so used to small amounts of food, they were warned that overeating too soon could make them very sick.

A newly appointed Polish Ambassador to the Soviet Union was appointed by General Sikorski to find the missing Polish officers. His name was Stanisław Kot.[xix] In April 1943, German intelligence were alerted to the discovery of eight large mass graves at a site in the Katyn Forest near Smolensk in Russia. Local people had been placing birchwood crosses at the site which revealed the burial of the Polish Army officers' bodies. The official Soviet statement about this discovery however, claimed that the mass shootings had been carried out by the German military, and that Nazi liars were spreading slanderous rumours that the Soviet Union had been responsible. General Sikorski demanded that Stalin tell him where the military prisoners were, as he knew they had been held at Kozelsk, Starobilsk and Ostashkov camps. Stalin repeated once again, that they had escaped into Manchuria, but Sikorski did not believe him. He did not believe that they were dead. The Red Cross were appointed by both the Polish and the German governments, but the Soviets would not give them permission to examine the graves. The massacre was in fact carried out by the NKVD under Beria's order, for which the murderers were awarded a 'financial bonus'[xx] for their work.[27]

Other mass burial pits were consequently found later in the century. Bodies of Polish officers were exhumed in the 1990s using archaeological methods, at Mednoye a village 126 miles north-west of Moscow, and

---

27 The Soviet Union did not accept responsibility until 2004 when it was investigated as a war crime. This investigation accepted that Stalin was responsible but refused to acknowledge the event as a war crime due to those accused being dead.

at Piatykhatky in Ukraine. Comprehending these massacres against the Polish military personnel is hard for me, but for Marian it must have been unimaginable, however, the details of these investigations may not have reached surviving Polish servicemen in Britain as the horrific war crimes were only admitted after Marian's death. Churchill and Roosevelt had become allies with Stalin in order to achieve victory over Nazi Germany. Although Churchill knew that Stalin was an evil dictator, he pretended publicly to defend the Soviet Union, and said that he would 'sup with the devil' if it led to victory over Nazi Germany so the news of the Polish massacre was suppressed in Britain.

General Sikorski died on 4 July 1943 in a mysterious plane crash, on take-off, in Gibraltar. Despite conspiracy theories that he was assassinated, the exhumation of his body 65 years after his death found no evidence that this was the case. However, there are many Polish people who believe that he became a barrier to the relationship between Churchill and Stalin and the Institute of National Remembrance, who investigate World War Two crimes, continue to investigate sabotage. A digital simulation of the take-off was created by Polish scientists in 1990 which showed that the Liberator plane that Sikorski was flying in 'was never out of control and the crash was faked'.[xxi]

CHAPTER 4

Marian trained with the 1st Parachute Brigade in various locations in Britain once he had recovered from his injuries. As well as his time at RAF Ringway he carried out training exercises in Dundee and Bara (Upper Largo). In August 1944 Marian was stationed at RAF Tarrant Rushton, in Dorset, awaiting instructions for his next military paratrooper mission. He encouraged Brian to visit a war memorial there as he explained how he had heard rumours that his brigade was going to be ordered to jump by parachute into Warsaw. This was in fact, to be an exclusive mission for the 1st Parachute Brigade, jumping into occupied Poland, however the British government instructed them to support the British 1st Airborne Division instead, leading to their involvement with Operation Market Garden in 1944.

Tarrant Rushton War Memorial

Marian must have felt homesick for Poland and would have been eager to hear news coming from Warsaw. He didn't see his family again after his capture in Poland in 1939 and told Brian that his mother and sister were killed during the Warsaw Uprising. This event was an incredible act of defence involving proud and patriotic Polish civilians who were still defending their homeland by resisting the wrath of the Nazi German invasion. The insurgence which was secretly planned by the Home Army (Armia Krajowa)[28] under the command of General Tadeusz Komorowoski, erupted into a battle of full-blown urban warfare. The Nazis had a plan for Warsaw and wanted to replace the existing city with a place where Aryanism[29] could thrive.

On 1 August 1944 men, women and children living in old Warsaw became citizen soldiers and supported a rebellion to help attack the German Army. The Poles had been secretly planning this uprising and had developed their own units of freedom fighters. Some weapons had been hidden in the city at the end of the Siege of Warsaw in 1939, before the Polish Army surrendered, but it was the tactical element of surprise that gave them the most advantage. The Germans were confused when they encountered these untrained fighters, who used this state of bewilderment to their advantage. In three days, the Polish freedom fighters used homemade petrol bombs and determined initiative, managing to secure the Wola district of Warsaw. The untrained army barricaded themselves into a safe area, using anything they could, including furniture and items from their homes. For several weeks they managed to keep a small pocket of Warsaw safe. However, the Polish uprising humiliated the German high command and the German Nazi leader, Heinrich Himmler, gave this explicit order:

'Every inhabitant must be killed; no prisoners are to be taken. Warsaw, is to be razed to the ground setting an example to the whole of Europe'.

The attack on the Polish citizens was led by the Secret Service Brigade and the ruthless Oskar Dirlewanger. The freedom fighters used the city sewers to try to outwit the Germans but eventually became overwhelmed and began to run short of ammunition. An appalling genocide began. The Polish fighters believed that help would come from their exiled government in London, but little support came for them.

---

28 Armia Krajowa was a large underground resistance movement made up of both military and political members including Polish citizens loyal to their government in exile.

29 The doctrine of the Nazi Party was biologically racist as they believed the Aryan race was superior to others.

At this time there was a British RAF base at Brindisi in Italy. Pilots based there were tasked with dropping supplies to the Polish fighters in the beleaguered city, but the command did not believe that they would have enough fuel be able to fly there and back. Captain Hugh Lunghi appealed to the Soviets for permission for them to base themselves in territory held by the Soviet Union Red Army, near to Warsaw, but he was not given permission. Eventually the RAF pilots did leave from Brindisi on desperate appeal from the Poles, but only just had enough fuel to make it back, causing them great anxiety.

Refusing permission for the planes to be allowed to base themselves in Soviet territory was a tactical plan by leader Stalin. Whilst he was implying to Churchill that they would be allies, he was in reality planning to take over Warsaw and Poland himself. The future of Poland had been conceded to the Soviets nine months earlier, and he did not want any allies coming to their aid. Winning the war against Germany was more of a concern to him, so that he could take over supreme control and when the Soviets finally entered Warsaw in 1945, a city in ruins, the liberators changed to oppressors and any of the freedom fighters who had survived, were killed or sent to Siberia.

The freedom fighters were isolated from all forms of support. Hopes were raised by a conscript of Polish soldiers, known as the Berling Army,[30] arriving in Warsaw. The Berling Army were fighting the Germans alongside the Red Army. The Allies were trying to get aid to the freedom fighters in the form of air drops, but the NKVD sabotaged

---

30 Some of the Polish officers who were imprisoned by the Soviet Union in three prison camps Kozelsk, Starobilsk and Ostashkov were not killed in 1940 unlike the majority. A group of high-ranking officers with impressive military talent were convinced by the NKVD that they should lead a Polish division in the Soviet Army. One of these men was General Zygmunt Berling. When Hitler signed a directive on 18 December 1940 that Germany would invade the Soviet Union leading to operation 'Barbarossa' Stalin needed the support of Polish Generals. The NKVD interrogating these men, led by Lavrentiy Beria, went to great lengths to persuade them to be disloyal to the Polish government in exile, sometimes by offering them luxury living conditions. A group of officers were housed in a Villa in Malakhovka where they received lavish hospitality to help convince them to agree to supporting the Soviet Union. Most were patriotic towards Poland and refused to agree to this, with one cavalry officer, Captain Narcyz Łopianowski, from the group saying that he would rather be shot than to conform.

this aid. Again, Polish hopes were raised when American planes were seen flying overhead, but most of the thousands of tonnes of aid they dropped fell into German hands. With the support of the Berling troops who were made up of mostly former farm workers, the freedom fighters continued to hold on to parts of Warsaw. For two months the soldiers fought with homemade ammunition and relied on seclusion by hiding in the sewers. The German soldiers were too scared to go into the filthy stinking sewers. Citizens who feared execution moved around the city before the start of the German curfew hours, to sleep with others overnight, to try to avoid arrest. Without any food or clean water to drink and surviving with only anguish and fear, the Polish fighters struggled to maintain their hold on Warsaw.

In August 1944, 40,000 Polish citizens were massacred, including Marian's mother and sister. The beautiful churches and most of the buildings in the city were reduced to rubble and during the first two days of invasion the German Luftwaffe destroyed nearly all the Polish aircraft.

On 2 October 1944 a ceasefire was negotiated with the Germans, with a concession that the Polish resistance would be treated as prisoners of war. Around 15,000 resistance fighters, both men and women, marched out of Warsaw, leaving behind them the bodies of their comrades. They left their dead as rotting corpses in the destroyed and broken city. Soon after the soldiers left 180,000 Polish citizens were ordered to leave the city. Many were killed by death squads, and others sent to concentration camps. After they left the German soldiers took to systematic ransacking, taking anything of valuable out of the homes and then setting light to the houses. The villages in Poland did not escape the terror of the German Nazi invasion either. Small villages and farm inhabitants were terrorised, many shot dead, and those who did

---

General Berling was successful in establishing a Polish military division within the Soviet Union and after the Sikorski–Mayski agreement was signed he was nominated to become the leader of this division becoming the commander of the 1st Polish Army until October 1944, hence its nickname the Berling Army. He refused to leave the Soviet Union with General Anders led an evacuation of troops and civilians from the country. These two Polish Generals hated one another.

not resist were taken prisoner. Their homes were looted, and thousands were loaded into unheated cattle trucks. Some of the homeowners were ordered to clean their homes first in preparation for German occupation. If you were a city dweller or a country farm resident, nobody was excused the wrath of the Nazi fascist orders.

I do not know when Marian learned of the death of his mother and his sister. He said that they were killed during these events of the Warsaw Uprising in August 1944.

In his book *Arnhem: The Battle for the Bridges, 1944*, Beevor compares Polish paratroopers to the British and identified that they were not only '*exiles fighting for the very survival of their national identity*' but also that the British did not really understand the people in Warsaw were suffering '*against impossible odds*' with the advancement of the Soviet Red Army.[xxii]

Beevor also wrote that the majority of British soldiers '*had heard only heroic accounts of Red Army prowess from newspapers and newsreels*' and did not have any knowledge of the Soviet treatment of Poland.[xxiii] It is unlikely, therefore that Marian knew anything about the deaths of his family members during his time at Tarrant Rushton.

The First Allied Airborne Army[31] was formed on 2 August 1944 on the command of General Dwight Eisenhower. A clash of personalities between the American and British commanders of this newly formed airborne army was not helped when the United States Airforce Lieutenant General Lewis Brereton was appointed as commander, leaving Lieutenant General Frederick Browning, who was the commander of the British Airborne Corps, to serve as his deputy. Browning was married to the author Daphne du Maurier, whose life had a trifling, but nonetheless interesting, connection with both Marian

---

31 The First Allied Airborne Army was created with six and a half divisions: The American XVIII Airborne Corps which managed the 82nd and the 101st Airborne Divisions along with the partially trained 17th Airborne Division, all of the British Airborne Divisions made up of the 1st and the 6th and the Polish 1st Parachute Brigade.

and Brian which will be revealed later in another chapter of this book.

The World War Two Operation Market Garden took place in September 1944, after the triumphant D-Day landings in June. It was a daring plan, coordinated by the British War Office to deposit 40,000 troops from the air, behind German enemy lines in Holland supported by ground forces, with the intention of capturing eight bridges that passed over canals on the Dutch border with Germany. General Bernard Law Montgomery formulated the plan, as it became clear to him that the soldiers on the ground fighting near Germany's borders were becoming isolated. Frontline troops who had pushed ahead to the Dutch frontier, began to run out of fuel and other supplies, due to an ever-increasing distance between them and backup support. Cargo could only be transferred across the English Channel into British-held ports such as Cherbourg. Beevor explains that *'With none of the Channel ports yet open, supplies had to be brought all the way from western Normandy in a constant shuttle, known as the "Red Ball Express"'.*[xxiv] Some cargo was getting through via Ostend and Dieppe, but it was very limited. Most of the existing railway network was destroyed, so replenishing ammunition, medical supplies and food was imperative if the ground forces were to remain effective.

Several previous air operations were planned after the successful invasion on D-Day, but these were postponed several times due to bad weather. Operation 'Comet' was aborted before 'Market Garden', involving British, American and Polish troops. The plan that was conceived was to drop airborne troops into the Dutch towns of Arnhem, Eindhoven and Nijmegen to capture bridges over the Dutch rivers supporting the land-based troops so they could advance simultaneously and liberate the Dutch towns.

Major General Sosabowski was put under operational command of the 1st Airborne Division by General Browning, so he reported to Major General Roy Urquart. They first met when several operations: Transfigure, Linnet Fifteen and Comet were conceived and subsequently abandoned in close succession. Sosabowski wrote in his own memoir,

Freely I Served,[xxv] that *'Browning made these plans with tremendous, perhaps dangerous confidence'* and that he thought that Browning's judgement of German opposition in the Arnhem area was optimistic. This comment was proven to be one of wise foresight.

The operation was planned in two parts, 'Market' was the code name for the air operation and 'Garden', the ground assault that was to advance towards Arnhem. British, Polish and American pilots were involved in the airborne part, which included engineless glider planes, which were towed behind aircraft, containing land support vehicles and artillery. Polish commander, Sosabowski, who's men were to be involved in the airborne operation had already aired his concerns that his brigade's part in an airborne operation would be a suicide mission as he was worried that there was a higher number of enemy forces in the drop zone areas than the British intelligence had suggested. On 15 September a build-up of German Panzer divisions in the Arnhem area was reported to the British commanders but after ignoring concerns from Major Brian Urquhart[32] (1st Airborne Corps Intelligence Officer) who had evidence of this being true, General Browning gave instructions for Operation Market Garden to go ahead. Operation 'Garden' was led by Lieutenant General Brian Horrocks.

On 17 September the ill-fated mission began, with troops having no knowledge of the reported presence of German troops in the area.

Marian's recollection of his involvement in Operation Market Garden, as he recounted to Brian of how he had jumped from a plane, with a parachute into Arnhem, are factually accurate, but in order to bring a bit more context into the realities of his life as a paratrooper, it is helpful to appreciate that the airborne troops spent quite a bit of time waiting for action before the operation began. Marian told Brian that at the last minute, when he assumed he was going to be given instructions

---

32 Brian Urquhart was born in Bridport in Dorset. (In the film *A Bridge Too Far* directed by Richard Attenborough, Brian Urquhart's character was renamed 'Major Fuller'(played by Sean Connery), to avoid confusion with the British Major General Robert Elliot 'Roy' Urquhart, who was the commander of the 1st Airborne Division in the Battle of Arnhem.)

to jump into Poland, he was told it would be Holland instead.

On the tape recording, Marian sounded as if he was pleased to be given the opportunity to take 48 hours leave. In an amused tone he revealed to Brian that he was

'a very naughty boy!'

His rather humorous account attracted the attention of one of the ward staff members, as a female voice can be heard on the tape, and she sounds very intrigued by what Marian was saying. Brian is heard explaining to the staff member that Marian was issued with five condoms and given a short period of off-duty leave. Marian must have been having such a good time with the ladies that he lost track of time and arrived back to the barracks late. He recounted how this had resulted in him being disciplined and that his 'stripes' were taken away as a penalty. In light of receiving this punishment he said that he was not permitted to fly in a glider, which was going to be part of the forthcoming Operation Market Garden. He was given orders to join the paratroopers who would be transported by plane. Marian's own words were:

'a little bit of sex, saved my life',

which may well have been true.

In England, 320 gliders took off from airfields in England with only 283 landing in the planned zones. Marian was acutely aware of Polish fatalities on that mission and realised that if it were not for his amorous few hours, he might well have been killed flying in a glider. The female ward staff member in Bournemouth Hospital agreed, that his leave was well timed. Marian was keen for Brian to know that he did get reinstated to his former rank at some point later. The waiting period for his involvement in the action dragged for Marian though, as the Polish paratroopers were scheduled to be a part of the Third Lift, which did not commence until 21

September 1944 due to delays caused by unsuitable weather.

The 1977 film *A Bridge Too Far*, directed by Richard Attenborough and based on a 1974 book written by Cornelius Ryan, describes in detail the how errors in mission Operation Market Garden were made, from fundamental communication problems to an explanation of how the Germans gained advantage after finding confidential paper plans for the operation in an abandoned glider. Beevor wrote that the Germans finding the plans meant that they *'revealed all the signals'*, giving them a tactical advantage.[xxvi] The whole operation was in fact beset with issues relating to poor communication.

One of the main objectives was to capture two bridges that spanned the River Waal in Nijmegen. On the sunny morning of Sunday 17 September 1944, the RAF Second Tactical Air Force attacked German barracks in the Netherlands and in north-western Germany. In what was referred to as the First Lift 1,544 transport planes and 478 gliders carrying 20,000 troops, involving the 1st Airborne Division, prepared to take off from air bases in the east and south of England, where they would be transported to the planned drop zones.[xxvii] Marian was not part of this First Lift, as I mentioned he was to take part in the Third Lift.

Some of these young paratroopers became overwhelmed with fear, which led to several of them deliberately damaging their own parachutes, so that they did not have to take part. This action, consequently, led to them having to face court-martial trials for cowardice. The Allied fighter planes attacked a large generator, cutting off the supply of electricity to the towns of Nijmegen and Arnhem and in the chaos of the bombing the Dutch people believed that liberation was imminent. Paratroopers preparing to jump were understandably very nervous, and the atmosphere inside all the aircrafts would have been tense. Some slept, others read their Bibles.[33] How these troops were feeling at

---

33 American and British soldiers were issued with pocket-sized versions of the New Testament and the Book of Psalms.

this time is hard to imagine, but accounts have been recorded of some paratroopers praying, crying, singing and harming themselves as they each managed to deal with a multitude of emotions. Camaraderie was subdued as each man considered their own mortality and contemplated the danger of their mission.

The thousands of parachutes falling out of the sky over Holland must have looked like dandelion seeds floating on the wind, as they made their descent after the paratroopers jumped from the aircraft. Some, like Marian, who had previously been injured in Tobruk would have had earlier experiences to dwell on, adding to the anxiety of the situation. The equipment that paratroopers carried matched their own weight, so they could not move about very easily. Along with the parachute, they also carried survival equipment and three days rations. *'Each 24-hour ration pack contained meat cubes, concentrated oatmeal, boiled sweets, plain chocolate, cigarettes, benzedrine tablets and a powder of tea-leaves, sugar and dried milk ready-mixed for the addition of hot water'*.[xxviii]

Sosabowski explains in his memoir that the brigade was divided into groups of 16–18 men who travelled in each aircraft. Each paratrooper carried their own personal equipment, but they also had kit bags attached to their legs containing radios, medical supplies and parts of machine guns.[xxix] The planes also carried bundles of equipment including folding bicycles.

Paratroopers jumped clutching heavy weapons, wearing helmets that were covered with camouflage netting and a traffic light system aboard the planes signalled when each paratrooper was to jump as they avoided *'slipping on the vomit and urine slopping around on the floor'*.[xxx] A close succession of timed jumps is referred to as a stick of paratroopers as they jump, aiming to land in a particular drop zone. During Operation Market Garden the aircraft flew from Britain via one of two routes, with the northerly route crossing a larger expanse of sea. The First Lift was successful with most of the troops landing where they were supposed to. The 101st American Airborne Division successfully captured four bridges as planned but the bridge at Son was blown up by the Germans before it could be taken. Part of the 1st British Airborne Division, landed near Oosterbeek in the afternoon. Some of these paratroopers defended the landing zone as more jumped. The 2nd Parachute Battalion commanded by Major General John Frost, marched his troop of 745 men towards Arnhem about eight miles away. He sent some of his troops to warn the occupants of the town that they should anticipate imminent fighting and advised them to evacuate their homes. They managed to capture the northern end of the bridge but not the southern one and he was expecting back up from the rest of the 1st Airborne Division, but radio problems meant that he could not communicate with them, so they became unsupported and surrounded by German Panzer Corps.

On the morning of the planned Second Lift on Monday 18 September, the weather in England was foggy so it was postponed for several hours. Gliders began arriving in the afternoon at a landing zone near the village of Son on the outskirts of Eindhoven. The 4th Parachute Brigade led by General John Hackett dropped at Ginkel Heath. The drop and landing zones were expected to be protected by the troops on the ground.

Towed Waco and Horsa gliders were used to carry paratroopers, land transport, anti-tank guns and ammunition. On take-off, the plane acted as a tug, pulling the flimsy gliders up into the sky. *'The glider, because it was so light, always tended to fly higher than the tow plane, which gave their occupants a chance to see the sky full of other aircraft'.*[xxxi] Due to their lightweight construction they were a dangerous form of transport and many succumbed to fatal damage from German flak[34] that was designed to deliver an explosion close by. If a glider survived its flight through enemy fire, then the landings were equally risky with many landing badly, injuring and sometimes killing those inside.

---

34 A type of anti-aircraft gunfire.

Others flipped over, sometimes crashing into other gliders that had landed successfully. Vehicles that were being transported inside the aircraft crushed some soldiers to death before they had a chance to get out. There were also farm animals to contend with too, cows grazing in the fields were startled by the sudden activity and ran in all directions as glider pilots tried to avoid them. You can see why Marian's dalliances in Tarrant Rushton may have saved his life!

At one landing zone near Wolfheze five gliders caught fire after they encountered German machine gun fire. Allied ground troops undertook the mission to retrieve the wounded and the dead and some were so badly injured that they begged their comrades to shoot them. Paratroopers also came under fire and men were killed before they got to the ground. Gliders also crashed into the sea, but due to their wooden construction they floated, making it possible to rescue many of the troops. The gliders that crash landed in enemy territory were hidden by the Dutch resistance inside haystacks, who also provided the pilots with bicycles and maps so that they could try and re-establish contact with their own forces. The 1st and 3rd Parachute Battalions from the Second Lift fought their way towards Arnhem but were a much-reduced force due to injury, death and capture.

The next day, 19 September 1944 was when Polish Parachute Brigade planned to join the 1st Airborne Division in Holland south of the Arnhem Bridge but bad weather and communication problems meant that things did not go to plan. Glider take-offs from Tarrant Rushton airfield were postponed as were the American and Polish paratroopers who were ready to board Dakota aircraft at Saltby and Spanhoe airfields.

In Holland the 14th Field Squadron (part of XXX Corps), built a Bailey Bridge[35] over the Wilhelmina Canal, so that troops and vehicles

---

35 Bailey Bridge, named after its designer Donald Bailey, is a modular construction made up of individual parts that were easily transportable.

could cross. The convoy made good progress on this misty morning, passing through the town of Veghel, as they headed towards the next bridge over the River Waal at Grave. At this same time American paratroopers of the 502nd Infantry Regiment were holding a defensive position near the bridge at Best after the Germans had blown it up. These soldiers had to surrender to the Germans after they ran out of ammunition, but not before their brave comrade, Joe Mann, had attempted to protect some of them from a grenade by shielding them with his own body. Mann was killed instantly.[36]

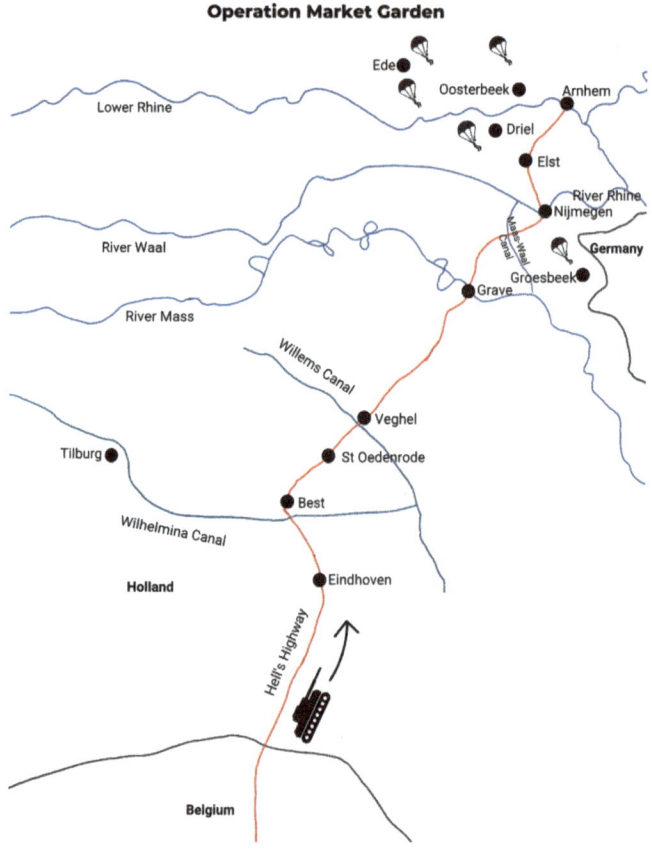

Operation Market Garden

---

36 There are two monuments dedicated to Joe Mann in Best – see Memorials list on page …

General Browning who had flown to Nijmegen by glider was concerned that he had been unable to make crucial radio contact with the 1st Airborne Division in Arnhem. He met with General Gavin and General Allan Adair and they agreed that they should try to take control of the bridges in Nijmegen, which were still held by the Germans. Nijmegen had both a road and a railway bridge that spanned the River Waal. The Allied force commanders were unaware that the German reinforcements were increasing in the area, and they expected them to withdraw when they attacked. General Gavin ordered that assault boats would attack the northern end of the bridge and was aware there was rumour that the Germans had control over a remotely wired plunger that might blow up the road bridge, located in the local post office. However, a detonator was not found by Allied troops when it was stormed. Dutch residents began to flee as the fighting escalated, and the Germans set light to their homes.[37]

When the planned Allied attack on the bridges in Nijmegen seemed destined for failure, General Gavin suggested that troops should attempt a daylight crossing of the River Waal, west of the bridges. The convoy of XXX Corps vehicles that were moving slowly along Highway 69 found themselves constantly under German attack and there were fierce battles at the towns of Sint-Oedenrode and at Best. The more recently constructed Bailey Bridge at Son was also attacked by German Panther tanks. It was two steps forward and three back at times as the coordination of Allied units, attempting to provide cover to one another was affected by the shortage of fuel and lack of backup from fresh paratroopers delayed in England by the weather.

---

37 Nijmegen had suffered from a catastrophic bombing raid earlier that year in February, when a large part of the city was destroyed by US Army aircraft when they targeted Nijmegen railway station in a secondary 'target of opportunity'. On 22 February 1944 aircraft involved in a planned bombing mission, took off from RAF Bungay air base in Suffolk to attack an aircraft factory in the German city of Gotha. It was a dangerous mission due to the length of the flights over German territory. The pilots were assigned a secondary target if Gotha could not be reached, so that the efforts and cost of the mission was not wasted.

In Eindhoven, citizens were premature in celebrating the expected liberation of their town, as during this September night Luftwaffe bombers attacked the city killing 227 civilians and wounding hundreds.

The following day 20 September paratroopers of the US 82nd Airborne Division landed in drop zones around the village of Groesbeek. The Allied units had secured the drop zones but met fierce resistance when they reached the outskirts of the city. The location of military units belonging to the German 10th SS Panzer Division made it impossible to access the Nijmegen bridges from the south. The arrival of the boats needed for the planned river crossing was delayed, and six out of the 32 were damaged by shelling. A group of officers including three generals, Browning, Horrocks and Gavin studied the banks of the River Waal from a power station building to determine the safest place to cross the fast-flowing river. Major Julian Cook, commander of the 3rd Battalion of the 504th Parachute Infantry regiment was appointed as the leader for the crossing, but the morale of the troops was not good as they did not believe that the mission would be successful, and it was considered suicidal. As this was a daytime operation the Leicestershire Yeomanry were ordered to provide smokescreen cover as the small canvas boats entered the water. With support cover from the Irish Guards, in Sherman tanks, Major Cook and his troops paddled furiously to attempt to cross the river. The smokescreen had limited effect and a hailstorm of bullets came down on the vulnerable soldiers. Climbing over the dead and wounded, some of the uninjured men returned to collect more troops in a second crossing. Out of 26 original boats, only 11 were stable enough to do this, as many had been hit and damaged or had sunk. Dutch civilians attempted to help the injured out of the river, but many soldiers' bodies floated past them.

The constant fighting in Nijmegen meant that a large part of the city was on fire and the flames reflected in the river. Many of Cook's troops who had survived the crossing, were wet and traumatised by the horrors of witnessing so many of their comrades killed but they courageously continued to take orders to attack the Germans on the north bank. Communication confusion indicated that 3rd Battalion had arrived at the railway bridge, when it was in fact the road bridge, which had been wired with explosive devices but was still intact when it was taken by the Allied forces. The explosive devices were disabled and the German soldiers trying to defend the bridge were killed, with some of them being run over by the tanks as they crossed the bridge. Nijmegen was liberated that day and the Germans in the town surrendered, but there were many casualties.

Major General Sosabowski, Marian's overall commander, was frustrated by the delays, ordering his men in the 1st (Polish) Independent Brigade to leave their stations in England and received very little information about what was happening in Holland.[xxxii] Orders were finally received at 8.45 am for them to land near the village of Driel, which is on the south side of the River Rhine. He suspected things had gone wrong, as the original plan was for three Polish parachute battalions to jump onto a drop zone south of Arnhem so that they could assist 1st Parachute Brigade with the defence of the bridge. Major General Frost's 2nd Parachute Battalion were holding the bridge, but maintaining this position looked doubtful.[38] Take-off for Sosabowski's men was subsequently delayed for another 24 hours due to more bad weather. The First Allied Airborne Army did attempt to drop supplies to the troops on the ground but most of these ended up in enemy hands as once again communication about a change of drop zone was not received!

Marian and the other Polish paratroopers received news on this day that Warsaw was falling to the Germans after relentless efforts from the Polish resistance. This must have been so demoralising for them when they knew that original plans were for them to be dropped in their own

---

38 Major General John Frost was badly injured during the defence of the Arnhem Bridge. In the film *A Bridge Too Far* he was portrayed by Sir Anthony Hopkins.

country. General Sosabowski was angry and stated that he would not take part in the operation if things were not explained to him as he knew that the situation had clearly changed. Beevor refers to the role of the Polish brigade as 'simply to help pull British Chestnuts out of the fire'.[xxxiii]

The ground offensive was 60 or so miles away from the descending 1st British Airborne Division as the morning of 21 September began. They needed to move 2,300 vehicles that were carrying equipment to build Bailey Bridges along with 9,000 engineers via the narrow road from Eindhoven towards Arnhem, but the conditions of the soggy low-lying highway and unexpected German resistance meant that they were delayed in connecting with the airborne troops as planned. This route became known as Hell's Highway which crossed polder land.[39] Troops from the 21st Army Group XXX Corps were under the command of Lieutenant General Brian Horrocks, who struggled to move forward due to constant attacks from Generalfeldmarschall Walter Model's Army. The troops became tired and were desperately hungry due to the RAF replenishment drops landing into German hands. Many of them were injured and in need of medical support. Those with serious injuries were given morphine, and their heads marked with blue ink so that others knew that they might be sedated and not dead, as they might have appeared. Troops were given a drug called Benzedrine, amphetamine sulphate that helped them to stay awake. German troops were issued with a different drug, Pervitin, a methamphetamine, which had the same effect as Benzedrine. Both these drugs are central nervous system stimulants and are more recently referred to as recreational drugs such as 'speed and rocket fuel'.

During the afternoon of 21 September after the weather conditions had finally improved 114 Dakota aircraft, carrying Marian and his fellow Polish paratroopers, finally took off from England. Some of them had to turn back as the weather was still causing havoc. The German

---

39 Polder is low-lying reclaimed land.

Luftwaffe shot down 13 planes, and more were damaged by anti-aircraft fire from the ground. Marian was one who jumped from one of the 53 aircraft, along with his Polish commander Major General Sosabowski. Cholewczynski's reference to one proud Jewish Pole gives an idea of these young men, who he wrote, did not all reflect the recruiting-poster image of a paratrooper:

'The man, however, possessed incredible spunk and spirit, and energy that was infectious'.[xxxiv]

Once they all reached the ground and untangled themselves from their parachutes, they headed to the Heveadorp Ferry, which they believed was in British hands, but it had in fact had been scuttled and was half sunk so they could not cross the Nederrijn.[40]

The following day on 22 September General Sosabowski recommended that Dutch citizens evacuate Driel. Some remained as they wanted to help the soldiers with their injuries. The General moved around the village on a lady's bicycle that he found in a farm.

General Urquhart's men in the British Airborne headquarters the Hotel Hartenstein in Oosterbeek were in a desperate situation and were continuously under fire from the Germans who had gradually closed in on the building. The German forces had also received orders from General Bittrich to kill the paratroopers that had landed in Driel and prevent any further Allies getting across the River Waal to reinforce the British in Oosterbeek.

The Dutch land where this fighting took place was very fertile, an area that produced a lot of fruit trees, so despite the lack of food, the Allied forces sometimes had the opportunity to pick fruit to eat. A comment made by a Polish private in Cholewczynski's book shows that despite the difficult conditions, some of the Polish soldiers maintained a sense of humour, referring to the good quality of the soil he said: 'you almost wouldn't mind being buried in it'.[xxxv] Most of the Polish paratroopers

---

40 Nederrijn is the name of the Dutch part of the River Rhine.

were dug in defensive fighting positions known as foxholes.

During the afternoon, plans were made for Polish paratroopers to attempt to cross the Nederrijn at night in rubber dinghies and rafts to provide vital reinforcements to the 1st Airborne Division in Oosterbeek. The British troops held only 400m of the riverbank, so they figured they could get 200 men across before the morning by using a hawser as the river current was very strong. The attempts to secure the thick rope failed so the boats that were swept downstream were at risk of being shot at and the soldiers killed, injured or captured. They didn't have any paddles for these dinghies, so they used shovels instead. They made two successful crossings before the Germans realised what was happening. Some dinghies sank as they were deflated by bullets and the soldiers were swept away into the river. One of the British platoons had been shooting at the Poles as they hadn't received information about the operation. Another communication misfortune!

Some of the Polish paratroopers who survived the river crossing took shelter on the morning of 23 September in Oosterbeek church, before they were met by the British troops.

Back in England at Spanhoe airfield more Polish paratroopers were preparing to board Dakotas as the weather had finally improved. There was some concern about the condition of the parachutes as they had become damp from the wet weather. Sosabowski was relieved to receive news that the planes carrying his paratroopers, who had turned back due to the weather conditions the previous day, were safe in England. In Driel the lack of boats needed for the river crossings for the paratroopers, who would be landing later in the day, was being discussed. It was agreed that 18 larger boats would be available at 20.00 hours along with Canadian sappers from the Wessex Division to help man them. The Dakotas took off mid-afternoon under the command of Major Marian Tonn along with 230 Waco gliders and the rest of the Polish paratroopers, some of whom were leaving for the second time.

German defences around Oosterbeek were attacked from the air with rockets by Typhoon planes and Stirling bombers dropped supplies including canned food over Driel. Paratroopers who jumped from the Dakotas and gliders landed in close succession in windy conditions. They needed to untangle themselves quickly as more gliders were scheduled to land soon after them. About 100 landed successfully with their contents of troops and anti-tank guns. Major Tonn was pleased to learn that the other part of the Polish brigade had crossed the river and reached Driel.

On Sunday 24 September 1944 a temporary ceasefire was agreed so that the wounded could be treated and civilians in Oosterbeek had a chance to flee the town. The arrival of the Polish reinforcement boosted the morale of the existing troops, but Sosabowski was concerned to see how tired and unwell many of the soldiers appeared. Due to the lack of food and shortages of water the soldiers were malnourished and exhausted. RAF Dakotas had been attempting to drop food parcels to the troops already on the ground, but they had to fly through heavy enemy fire, and often the packages ended up in German hands.

The progress of the vehicles moving along Hell's Highway was slow, and medical supplies were not getting through to those who needed them. DUKW vehicles known as Ducks were six-wheeled amphibious transport, that were designed as both a truck and a boat, became bogged down in mud. The 4th Battalion of the Dorsetshire regiment, led by Lieutenant Colonel Gerald Tilly, was ordered to cross the Nederrijn to assist in the operation to evacuate the airborne division who were still trapped on the Arnhem side. That night the 4th Battalion of the Dorsetshire Brigade, along with the recently landed Polish paratroopers, planned to cross the river so the Polish sappers marked the loading area on the riverbank with white tape as soon as it was dark. However, not all the boats that they needed and had been promised, arrived as some were captured and others that were being transported on trucks got stuck on the boggy road. It was in the early hours of the morning when six boats eventually turned up. These boats carried 12 passengers. Cholewczynski describes them as FB Type-3 assault boats[xxxvi] that had been used previously for the crossing of the River Waal. These had a plywood floor and canvas sides. Just as before, a strong current was flowing in the river, making the crossing just as challenging and once again the soldiers' used spades and rifle butts as paddles to steer the small boats through the water. They were under constant fire from Germans troops, but with some retaliation from XXX Cops artillery regiments. The Dorsets led the crossing attempt. Unfortunately, due the current that was sweeping the little boats downstream, Lieutenant Tilly's boat landed on the northern riverbank, but behind enemy lines. Troops continued to attempt to cross the river, in the small boats, all through the night but there was a high loss of life both on the water and on the riverbank. Some of the soldiers ended up in the water and swam for their lives. Lieutenant Colonel Gerald Tilly was wounded and realised his position was hopeless as he and his crew were completely outnumbered, so they surrendered. They were taken as POWs. Lieutenant Leo Jack Heaps, a Canadian serving in the British Army was one of those who ended up in the water before being captured:

'The water of the Rhine felt warm as I drifted easily far out into the swift stream. At the ferry crossing the Germans continued to aim an unending barrage of mortars at me which crashed down on the landing road. Factories flamed along the banks of the Rhine like burning pyres, and the river reflected the yellow smoky clouds. I swam westward with the current. A piece of driftwood struck me in the back and I reached out and held on. Perhaps half an hour later my feet touched bottom as I came back to the north shore. Unmistakable German voices and marching boots crushed the earth above me. A column of troops was going east. I crawled onto the grass and waited. German machine guns arced long beads of red tracers overhead. The prospect of becoming a prisoner was not very appealing and I chose to push out again into the water. I suppose I thought if I stayed in the river long enough I would float out through Moerdijk to the sea. The idea was quite preposterous, but this is what I thought would happen. I do not know how many hours I floated in the

Rhine, but I passed burning factories and houses on boat shores. When the current deposited me again on the north bank I was many miles west of the Oosterbeek perimeter. The sky to the east had a tiny touch of pink that shone through the murk and smoke that obscured Arnhem'.[xxxvii]

Heaps was given civilian clothing after his capture as he was only wearing mud-caked underwear when he was arrested, and luckily for him the army issue dog tag that would have revealed his number name and religion had fallen off. Heaps was Jewish. He later escaped from the Germans by jumping from the cattle car of the train he was being transported on, which led to him working closely with the Dutch resistance before he became reunited with his comrades.

I cannot be absolutely sure on which date Marian was in one of the boats on the river, but he survived! He mentioned rubber boats, so it was more likely that it was on 22 September 1944. He told Brian that he had managed

'three overs, and a swim',

meaning that he had managed to cross the river in the rubber dinghy several times. He said

'they wanted very badly medicine in Oosterbeek'

but realised that he could not do any more as he had been wounded again! Marian said to Brian that he wished he had not been there and although his job on the river was extremely dangerous he knew how important it was to deliver important pain-relieving drugs to the injured troops. Brian had spent much of his life aboard small boats and was familiar with the challenges of rubber dinghies, so would have appreciated how a shot fired at the hull would cause the boat to deflate and sink quickly. Marian confirmed that three boats were destroyed but was proud that he had managed three delivery trips before he was wounded.

A Polish Voice

It was raining on 25 September, which cannot have helped the mood of General Urquhart when he had to take the decision to try to evacuate the remaining 1st Airborne Division, who were trapped in German-held territory on the north of the Nederrijn, with seriously depleted quantities of ammunition and food. He requested that his officers should not announce operation 'Berlin'[41] to their troops until late in the day, so that this hazardous plan had the maximum chance of success. At the Polish operation headquarters in Driel, Sosabowski was informed that the Polish paratroopers, who had been the last to arrive in the area should therefore be the last to leave to provide military cover, whilst the other troops attempted to cross the Nederrijn in small canvas boats. Beevor explains in his book that *'this was a particularly bitter moment'* for the Polish paratroopers as they had *'not been in Warsaw fighting alongside their compatriots'*.[xxxviii] Many of those killed in Oosterbeek were buried there by comrades. The rain that day did at least provide the soldiers with drinking water, as the limited supply that they possessed was being saved to be given to injured soldiers. Beevor recorded accounts of paratroopers experiencing nervous breakdowns and even a suicide in a slit trench. Remaining positive to the task in hand was clearly challenging, as so many men were being killed. The details of Operation Berlin were shared at 17.50 and began as darkness fell, with British and Canadian troops attempting to transport men across the river in the collapsible assault boats. These small craft were fitted with outboard motors, but the engines did not always start easily in the rainy conditions, and the strong river current swept the lightweight boats downstream. Back and forth the little boats went, attempting to rescue as many troops as possible. They were under constant enemy fire, but the low level of the riverbank meant that the large German machine guns could not aim at the soldiers in the water. Some of the men decided

---

41 Operation Berlin (25–26 September 1944) was a planned night-time evacuation of the 1st Airborne Division from German occupied territory on the north bank of the Nederrijn.

to try to swim as those who had not yet been rescued feared daylight would prevent them from getting into one of the little boats as they waited for their turn. Panic drove some of them to overload the boats causing them to capsize. Marian told Brian that he had swum across the river during the night and that he had pushed a body out of his way. It is not possible to know how severe his injury was, and if it happened during Operation Berlin or on the previous day. Many soldiers ended up in the water, some accidentally and some purposefully. The river crossing in the boats was hazardous, some thought that swimming across gave them a better chance of avoiding enemy fire. Those who did reach safety on the Driel side of the riverbank were cold and exhausted but managed to follow '*a white guide tape over a muddy dyke*' and were given a mug of hot tea in a barn where they were met by comrades who dealt with the wounded.[xxxix] The strength of the original force of Allied forces who took part in Operation Market Garden was severely depleted. The bodies of dead soldiers drifted down stream, many were recovered and collected by the Red Cross for burial.

Operation Berlin was eventually aborted due to heavy German gunfire, leaving many soldiers trapped on the wrong side of the river with no option other than to surrender. There were several glider pilots who had survived and were hiding in woods. They were rescued by Canadian Royal Engineers, who managed to get them across the river.

The morning of 26 September 1944 was quiet in Oosterbeek as the gunfire stopped. The Germans ordered any civilians who were left in the town to leave. This was a disappointing day for the Dutch people as only a few days previously they had believed that they were about to be liberated. It was also a dangerous time for them as so many of them were involved with resistance support. Oosterbeek had been under a fusillade of heavy shelling, it was a broken town, and soldiers who had been hiding in cellars were taken as prisoners by the Germans and were marched into Arnhem.

On the other side of the river in Driel, Sosabowski and his uninjured

A Polish Voice

Polish paratroopers marched back towards Nijmegen after being refused the use of transport trucks[xl] by General Browning.[42]

St Elizabeth Hospital in Arnhem was used throughout the battle and became the base for the 16th Parachute Field Ambulance. Dutch, British and German medics, along with Red Cross personnel, treated all soldiers who were admitted while the fighting continued to rage nearby. Alexander Lipmann-Kessel parachuted into Arnhem as a surgeon with the 16th (Parachute) Field Ambulance, a Jewish South African serving as a Captain in the Royal Army Medical Corps. He described the hospital as 'ecclesiastical'[xli] as it was formerly staffed by an order of German nuns so many of its decorations were religious ones. Some civilian casualties were transferred to the small Dutch Reformed Church hospital, Diakonessenhuis, which the Germans used before it was completely destroyed in 1945. The Hotel Schoonoord in Arnhem was quickly converted into a medical facility by the owner's daughter Hendrika Van Der Vlist, and the nearby Hotel Tafelberg was used for emergency surgery.

Marian was admitted to St Elizabeth Hospital in Arnhem. I do not know on which day this happened and the exact circumstances. He remembered receiving an injection and being treated by an English doctor. He thought that he had been carried into hospital by a Dutchman and that he received morphine. He was in the hospital when the Germans began to take over. He said that he had heard rumours that the patients were going to be captured as prisoners of war, so he decided to try to escape. He told Brian that he had stitches so he must have received some surgical treatment. Marian's words were,

---

42 The relationship between these two men was not good and eventually led to General Browning writing a letter to Sir Ronald Weeks, Deputy Chief of the Imperial General Staff at the War Office in Whitehall criticising Sosabowski's attitude during operation 'Market Garden' and suggesting that he be removed from command of the 1st Polish Independent Paratroop Brigade. The consequence of this letter was Sosabowski's dismissal.

A Polish Voice

'Oh came out of the window to a low balcony and said oh that's my chance'.

He made his way to the river which was close to the hospital and met up with a Dutchman who helped him by redressing his wound. Marian said the Germans were oblivious to his escape and described them as

'bloomin' drinking and singing'

from a hotel nearby. Three injured officers who were admitted to the St Elizabeth Hospital also managed to escape. The first was Brigadier Gerald Lathbury, commander of the 1st Parachute Brigade, who had been injured in his back.[xlii] Also, General Hackett, wounded in his stomach and thigh, who was nearly given a lethal injection due to the severity of his injuries by a German doctor but received lifesaving surgery from Alexander Lipmann-Kessel,[xliii] known by his nickname during the war as Lippy. Whilst in the hospital the British doctors removed any indication of Hackett's senior rank and recorded him as Corporal Hayter[xliv] in the records for fear of any interrogation. Major Digby Tatham-Warter, commanding the 2nd Parachute Battalion, found it difficult to remember passwords so he carried an umbrella as a form of identification. He was injured several times and made his escape with his second in command, Captain Antony Frank, through a window the same way Marian did but they did not head towards the river, but instead to a wood. Many of these escapees were assisted by Dutch civilians, who hid them in their gardens, whilst waiting for support from the underground resistance operation who helped them to become reunited with their units.

Marian's escape was not made alone, there were other soldiers who considered swimming across the River Rhine in an attempt to escape capture from the Germans. The allied troops who were caring for the patients in the hospital knew they would probably be moved to a British-administered hospital in Apeldoorn or would be taken to prisoner of war camp if they were well enough. The Dutch resistance volunteers made many suggestions for hiding men before they were moved. One of these men was Hackett who was disguised as an injured civilian. He was smuggled out of the hospital into a Red Cross car 'bent half double due to weakness' as his stomach surgery was far from healed.[xlv]

After receiving some help from a man that he met, who turned out to be a Dutch Red Cross volunteer, Marian attempted to swim across the river during the night. He mentioned that the river was

'*very, very fast*',

referring to the strong current which pushed him sideways. Marian remembered seeing a small cottage when he reached the other side. He was assisted by the occupants of this cottage, who helped him to get dry. He was able to communicate with them in English as they both spoke a little. Brian asked Marian if he had any weapons with him at this point, as he wondered how he would have swum with them. Marian told him he

'only had one grenade in case'.

Marian was hidden by farmers who were part of the Dutch resistance, a strong underground movement who 'concentrated on helping those in danger with fake identities and ration books, as well as collecting intelligence for the Allies and passing shot-down pilots along escape lines through Belgium and France to Spain'.[xlvi] Marian spoke of these people as being '*so clever*' and explained to Brian how they had hidden him in their garden.

'They hide me in the bushes, dig hole, and I lie down like a rabbit under cover. They brought me food during the night, you know early morning'.

Brian was surprised to learn that Marian had been hidden like this for many uncomfortable days. He did not remain in the same place though. Marian told him *'Always move, never stop in one place too long'*. One of these hiding places that Marian mentioned was in a space that had been used to store manure for the farm. He described a waterlogged hole that the farmer had warned him that getting out of might have been challenging. The smelly hiding place was somewhere that Marian had clearly not forgotten about, neither was his injury, which he described to Brian as turning septic:

'not bleeding, only open, you know horrible yellow stuff'.

This was probably the wound that had been stitched in the St Elizabeth Hospital. Not only was his life at risk again by being discovered by the German soldiers, but he was also only just surviving by hiding in squalid places. He was told by the concerned Dutch farmers that it was too dangerous for him to remain where he was:

'older man and older lady, they say look, too much danger here for you, the best way we get you away from here. They say we clean and wash you and dry and giving you little bit something to eat, and they got the bread to share with me. I don't know name; he spoke so quick and fast. Dutch resistance he say well we going to have chance to contact American tonight. He said if you put a flag in the morning, don't go immediately'.

Brian asked him what sort of flag he meant. Marian replied:

'Oh white flag, but don't go immediately, they gonna shoot.'

He was describing the moment that he had tried to make his presence known to American troops. Brian would have only been 10 years old at this time but had experienced meeting American troops in his hometown of Weymouth in Dorset as they had arrived in the town during the winter of 1942. Dorset was a temporary home to thousands of American troops. His memories of American troops were of friendly soldiers who were kind and generous towards children, sharing their sweets, and he often spoke of being given chewing gum to try for the first time. Marian was wearing uniform when he was finally safe in the hands of American troops, but this did not happen without a few bullets being fired at him first. His clothes would have been filthy, from all the places that he had been hiding in during the weeks leading up to this. Marian said that from here he was cleaned up, fed and medically treated before being sent to Brussels, then back to England.[43]

Operation Market Garden was a very ambitious plan that was beset with communication challenges, bad weather and an optimistic assumption that the German resistance would be less than it actually turned out to be. There were more British casualties in this offensive than there had been on D-Day.

For the Dutch people, the airborne landings that began on 17 September, had '*generated immense excitement among the civilian population*' as they anticipated Allied victory and liberation.[xlvii] However, the reality was that the Germans' victory in holding control of Arnhem split the Netherlands in two, with only the southern half experiencing liberation. The occupants of Arnhem and those living in the north experienced severe brutality and retribution from the Nazi regime. Arnhem had previously been a prosperous picturesque town, with a civil and democratic society. The only Dutch authorities that were permitted to operate were the Red Cross, who were given orders to evacuate Arnhem. They were told that if these orders were not carried out then instructions would be given for the carpet bombings to be carried out. Around 150,000 civilians were ejected from the city before buildings were looted and then

---

43 The length of time Marian was hiding in the Dutch people's garden is not known, however a witness statement in Chapter 5 indicates that it could have been several weeks.

destroyed. This order, which has since been regarded as a war crime, was the subject of much speculation as to who gave it.

Lipmann-Kessel described Arnhem as he was trying to negotiate the transfer of his patients from the St Elizabeth Hospital:

'A grey drizzle and the absence of civilians added extra sadness to the glimpses of violent destruction. Ruins from bombing rapidly begin to get a mature look, but these streets of shattered, gutted houses seemed caught, as if by a camera, in their first astounded agony. Wrecked jeeps, blown-up tanks and pieces of artillery, broken looted shop windows, a splash of blood against a door, odd helmets, part of a booted torn-off leg overlooked by the grave diggers. In the main Square, monstrous tangles of overhead wires lay half across the road, and for a moment I saw the blackened, jagged remains of what had been buildings near the bridge where so many of the Second Battalion had died. We left the cadaverous streets and turned along the Apeldoorn road'.[xlviii]

The country then experienced what became known as the 'Hunger Winter' which was due to a combination of a non-existent rail network and the Germans forbidding any transportation of food for the Dutch people, which led to the deaths of 18,000 civilians who 'had been reduced to eating tulip bulbs in an effort to avoid starvation'.[xlix] The medical professionals who tried to treat the sick, mostly with cases of oedema, were desperately trying to maintain they own food intake on their meagre rations. Skin diseases were rampant and epidemics of diphtheria and typhoid spread quickly. The death rate rose so rapidly that undertakers could not manage to bury all of the dead. Henri van der Zee records in his book *The Hunger Winter* that a visitor to a cemetery in Rotterdam claimed *'The shrunken bodies were lying next to each other. No flesh on thighs or calves. Most had bent arms and legs, the hands clenched as if the poor devil was still asking for food'.*[l]

The famine was eventually eased with flour from Sweden and Allied food air drops brought in via humanitarian mercy flights permitted by the German forces.

After Christmas 1944 Marian was taken to Blatherwycke House near Kettering and Peterborough, where other Polish soldiers were stationed. He told Brian that he became an instructor for younger recruits. He met up with others from his regiment but said that there were just three of them that had returned from Arnhem.

Later in that year in a tent on Lüneberg Heath, south of Hamburg, a delegation of German high command signed a surrender document, following Hitler's suicide on 30 April. This was witnessed by Field Marshal Montgomery on 4 May 1945 at 18.30 hours. The war was over!

Marian remembered being gathered in Hyde Park in London at this time with other Polish troops who were moved via the Hook of Holland and sent to Germany.

The displacement of the Polish people took many years to resolve, and Europe was in chaos. In his book *How War Came*, Watt wrote '*In May 1945, Europe was near death*'.[li] Marian would have returned to a broken Europe. With transportation systems destroyed, railway tracks wrecked by bombs, bridges ruined, any journey would have been a challenge. Thousands of displaced people were trying to survive, and new beginnings would take years to nurture. The Polish troops were needed to oversee this, and Marian explained to Brian that he was moved around from camp to camp. The former German concentration camps were used as refugee centres.

Germany was divided into four zones of occupation and each zone was governed by one of four allied powers, the United States, the Soviet Union, Great Britain and France with the intention of restoring democracy. As these plans were being made more than 10 million Europeans were on the move. Emergency centres were set up in ex-prisoner of war camps so that refugees could find shelter and receive medical care. Polish Army units such as Marian's were stationed in the British occupation zone. The Polish 1st Parachute Brigade worked in the area of the town of Haren in the district of Emsland on occupational duties until 1947 when they were demobilised in June 1947. This city was renamed Maczków during the years of 1945 until 1947 after the Polish tank commander Stanisław Macez.

A Polish Voice

A Polish Voice

Marian spoke of meeting the United Nations dispersion people. He said they were categorising the Polish exiled people. On 18 July 1948 he was given the opportunity to return to England under the terms of the Polish Resettlement Act of 1947. This was immigration legislation that gave over 200,000 Polish troops the opportunity to live and work in Britain. This was a good decision on his part as the territorial changes under Joseph Stalin's rule meant that many Polish citizens found themselves living within different border zones than they did before the beginning of the war. German, Czechoslovakian and Polish borders were all affected by the 1945 border agreement that was signed between Poland and the Union of Soviet Socialist Republics (USSR).

During the 1950s and 1960s many of the former 'Armia Krajowa' members were deported to gulags and prison camps and higher-ranking members were executed.

A Polish Voice

KWESTIONARIUSZ OSOBISTY   QUESTIONNAIRE FOR POLISH RECORDS   3657   **POUFNE**

Kwestionariusz dołączyć do dokumentów ewidencyjnych, jeżeli są w oddziale, w przeciwnym wypadku oddzielnie przechowywać. Oddział wprowadza bieżące zmiany.

1. Kwestionariusz ten wypełniają wszyscy żołnierze Polskich Sił Zbrojnych bez różnicy stopnia oraz także zatrudnieni pracownicy cywilni, mężczyźni i kobiety, którzy nie życzą sobie obecnie powrócić do Polski.
2. Wypełnienie tego kwestionariusza w niczem nie narusza prawa ubiegania się o powrót do Polski w jakimkolwiek czasie.
3. Kwestionariusz ten ma wyłącznie na celu dostarczenie Władzom Brytyjskim koniecznych informacji i nie daje żadnych gwarancji, że wyrażone w nim życzenia będą spełnione.

A.—DANE OSOBISTE.

1. Nazwisko: ROGUSKI
   Imiona: MARIAN
2. Imię Ojca: JOZEF
3. Panieńskie Nazwisko/Tylko Mężatki/
4. Mężczyzna / Kobieta
5. Stopień Wojskowy Polski / Brytyjski
6. Nr. Ewidencyjny Wojsk Polski / Brytyjski
7. Stosunek do Służby Wojskowej
8. Data Urodzenia: Dzień 11 Miesiąc 2 Rok 1922
   Miejsce Urodzenia i kraj: WARSZAWA POLSKA
9. Obywatelstwo: POLSKIE
10. Kawaler/Panna — Zonaty/Zamężna — Rozwiedziony/na — Wdowiec/wa
    Ilość Dzieci:
11. Kategoria Zdrowia: A
14. Nr. poczty polowej oddziału:
15. Prywatny stały Adres:

12. Czy jesteś Członkiem Stowarzyszenia Polskich Kombatantów: NIE
    Podaj numer legitymacji Członkowskiej
13. Podaj numer twego koła Stowarzyszenia Polskich Kombatantów?

B. WYKSZTAŁCENIE CYWILNE

16. Podaj datę opuszczenia ostatniej szkoły lub uczelni wyższej: 1936

Nazwa szkoły powszechnej, średniej lub wyższej, gdzie	Przedmiot główny lub specjalność	Rodzaj uzyskanego świadectwa lub stopnia naukowego	Uczęszczał od-do
6. KLAS POWSZECH		UKON. 6 KLAS	1929-36

17. Kursy dokształcające

Czego uczyłeś się	Nazwa kursu i nazwa instytucji, organizującej	Uzyskane świadectwo lub złożony egzamin	Czas uczęszczania

W wojsku:

18. Jakimi obcemi językami mówisz lub piszesz? *ANGIELSKIM*

C. PRACA ZAWODOWA

Pracodawca /firma/	Co robiłeś?	Płaca	Daty zatrudnienia od-do
GOSPODARSTWO-ROLNE	*ROLNIK*		*1936-39*

19. Które z tych zajęć było twym głównym zawodem? *OGRODNICTWO*

Wymień dokładnie czynności, które w tym zawodzie wykonywałeś? *PIELĘGNO-WANIE DRZEW OWOCOWYCH*

28 29	Obecny pracodawca lub nazwa szkoły /uczelni/	Zajęcie lub przedmiot nauki /specjalność/	Data rozpoczęcia pracy lub czas ukończenia studiów	Zezwolenie brytyjskie od-do

D. UMIEJĘTNOŚCI DODATKOWE

22. Czy umiesz prowadzić samochód [TAK / **NIE**]   Czy umiesz prowadzić motocykl [TAK / **NIE**]

Podkreśl, co potrafisz z pewną wprawą dzięki zamiłowaniu lub pracy zawodowej:

a. Rysować   e. Naprawiać zegarki
b. Malować   f. <u>Uprawiać warzywa lub kwiaty</u>
c. Naprawiać instalacje elektryczne   g. Gotować
d. Naprawiać radio   h. Naprawiać obuwie

Na jakim instrumencie potrafisz grać? ....

Wymień inne twoje umiejętności ....

E. SŁUŻBA WOJSKOWA

23	Oddział	Funkcja	Stopień	Czas od-do
	Dyon ART P.PANC.	*OBSŁUGA-DZIAŁA*	*STRZ*	*42-47*

24. Data wcielenia do Polskich Sił Zbrojnych pod D-twem Brytyjskim:

Data *10.III 1942*   Kraj *ANGLIA*

A Polish Voice

F. INNE INFORMACJE

25. W jackich krajach przebywałeś dłżej, niż przez jeden rok?

Kraj	Czas pobytu	W jakim charakterze?	25
ROSJA	1940-1941	WIEZIEN	
NIEMCY	1945-1947	ŻOŁNIERZ	

7. Czy posiadasz/łeś brytyjskie dokumenty osobiste wojskowe lub cywilne TAK | NIE

Wymień jakie | ARMY BOOK 64 | 7

32. Podaj kraj i miejsce stałego zamieszkania w sierpniu 1939 r.? | WARSZAWA POLSKA | 32

26. Czego mógłbyś uczyć lub być instruktorem?

Przedmiot	Na jakim poziomie?	26

Czy masz już doświadczenie w nauczaniu lub instruowaniu? TAK | NIE

Uwagi: Poniżej możesz podać wszelkie inne informacje, które uważasz za ważne. Jeśli zabrakło ci miejsca na jakąkolwiek odpowiedź, możesz uzupełnić ją tutaj. | 36

H. PRZYSZŁOŚĆ

Nie należy odpowiadać na poniższe pytanie, jeżeli wypełniłeś p. 27, dotyczący twojej rodziny.

Możesz tu podać później zmianę twych zamiarów:

Kogo z członków rodziny chciałbyś zabrać ze sobą?

Nazwisko i imię	Wiek	Płeć	Stosunek pokrewieństwa	Gdzie teraz przebywa	27

Nazwisko żołnierza .... Imiona ....

Ewid. Wojsk. Nr. .... Oddział ....

Jeżeli tę część kwestionariusza żołnierz wypełnił po zakończeniu akcji spisowej, oddział uzupełni p. 27 i rubryki 30, 31, 33 kwestionariusza i prześle go do:— POLISH GENERAL STAFF, RECORDS OFFICE.

If this section has been detached from the questionnaire and completed after the interview, Units will enter the information in Section 27 and in boxes 30, 31 and 33 and send this section to:—POLISH GENERAL STAFF RECORDS OFFICE,

G. RODZINA

27.

Imiona żony/męża i dzieci	Płeć	Stosunek pokrewieństwa	Data urodz.	Kraj w którym przebywa	Czy chciałby zabrać ze sobą

Nazwisko i imię			Wiek		
					TAK
					TAK
					TAK
					TAK
					TAK

34. Ile Posiadasz? (1) Więcej niż £200   (2) £200 lub mniej

30	(1)
	(2)
31	(1)
	(2)
33	(1)
	(2)
	(3)

Podpis ...BOGUSKI...   Data ...6.V.1947...

Nazwisko referenta spisowego ...J. ORŁOWSKI...

H. PRZYSZŁOŚĆ

NAMYSL SIĘ DOBRZE ZANIM ODPOWIESZ NA TO PYTANIE. Możesz je narazie pominąć a dopiero później po zastanowieniu się poprosić twego przełożonego o ten arkusz, aby wpisać tutaj odpowiedź.

30. Jaką pracę wybrałbyś po demobilizacji, jeżeli nie będzie możliwe żadne szkolenie zawodowe?

(1) ROLNICTWO   (2) OGRODNICTWO

30. Kod (1) .... (2) ....

31. Gdybyś miał możność szkolić się zawodowo, jakiego zawodu cywilnego chciałbyś się nauczyć

(1)   (2)

31. Kod (1) .... (2) ....

33. W jakich krajach chciałbyś się osiedlić

	Kraj	Na własną rękę (z rodziną)	W polskiej Gromadzie	Kod 33
(1)	CANADA	TAK	NIE	
(2)				
(3)				

Nazwisko Referenta Spisowego
J. ORŁOWSKI

Podpis ...BOGUSKI...   Data 6.V.1947   Data 6.5.1947

CHAPTER 5

After Marian had taken the decision to live in England in 1948, he agreed to work for the government for five years. In this next chapter, you will learn about the difficulties he encountered living and working as a civilian. The ever-resourceful Marian maintained his sense of humour, despite his traumatic life in service with the Polish military.

As he possessed numerous skills, he explained how he was initially employed by the Fitzwilliam family, who lived at Milton Hall, near Peterborough in Cambridgeshire. Marian worked under the instruction of Mr Grimwade, as a groom in the stables at Longthorpe Manor, and then later trained as a chauffeur. He was sent on a chauffeur training course with Rolls-Royce, as their highly esteemed white glove training programme not only taught driving skills, but also appropriate dress code and etiquette. The Rolls-Royce chauffeur training teaches drivers how to drive the vehicles as smoothly as possible so that passengers are transported with the ultimate of comfort. Marian proudly told Brian that he had

'passed first class'.

He would have been issued with a chauffeur's uniform and needed to practise discretion about the identity of his passengers. He remembered collecting distinguished visitors from the railway station and said that he was expected to do more than just driving work for his employer! Marian cast his mind back, and laughing, told Brian that he had to ensure his boss got safely home and remembered on one occasion, having to help put him to bed after he had had too much to drink. It is not clear who he was referring to here though, Earl Fitzwilliam, Mr Grimwade or another member of the classy household. It sounded though as if

Marian enjoyed this work, which is not surprising as compared to his service history, this job must have been like a dream.

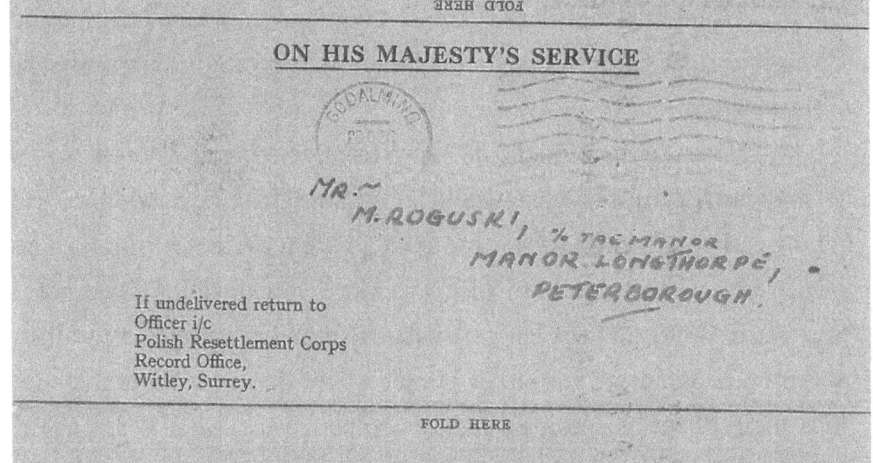

Milton Park is about three miles from Peterborough, with Milton Hall being the largest private house in Cambridgeshire. The land on which the house stands was bought in 1502 by a wealthy merchant from Yorkshire, William Fitzwilliam and was at that time part of Northamptonshire.

The estate, built by the Fitzwilliam family, remained the home of generations of William Fitzwilliam's ancestors and was the residence of the 10th Earl Fitzwilliam and his wife from 1904 until 1995 before it passed to another family. Milton Hall was used during both World Wars, as an auxiliary hospital in World War One and parts of the house and the stables were used in World War Two by the Czechoslovak Army and later by the secret war department, known as the Special Operations Executive, that was involved in classified operations in Europe such as reconnaissance, sabotage and espionage. The author Daphne du Maurier visited the house in 1917, as a child with her family and revealed in correspondence between her and Lord Fitzwilliam 20 years later, that the interior of 'Manderley' that she describes in her novel *Rebecca* was based on her memories of Milton Hall. Had Brian known of this connection, he maybe would have told Marian that he also had a connection with Mrs du Maurier.

Dad used to tell me stories about his youth, and I know that he slept aboard Daphne du Maurier's yacht as a young man when assisting the Commodore of Castle Cove Sailing Club in Weymouth, Dorset. Here is the story:

Mrs Gwendoline Wingfield-Digby from Sherborne, Dorset was a formidable lady in her seventies, who became the Commodore of the sailing club in 1945 and spent time in an adjacent cabin near the sea. She owned several boats, one of which was a small yacht called 'Fortunette'. She asked Brian to help her sail it back from Fowey in Cornwall to Weymouth. She drove him to St Mawes where they rowed out the boat in a small collapsible folding dinghy. Fortunette was a small ketch, about 19 ft long, with a centreboard rather than a fixed keel. They sailed the boat east, past Dodman Point, to Fowey where they moored in the river. Mrs Wingfield-Digby told Brian that she had to go to London so left him in charge of the boat. Brian got chatting to an 'old salt' who was aboard a 40-ft ketch which was moored nearby. Unsurprisingly, Brian, who seemed to make friends with most people he met during his life, made an acquaintance with the sailor. He was a professional skipper responsible for the yacht 'Jeanne D'Arc'[44] and suggested to Brian that he moor the little Fortunette alongside the bigger yacht, as the weather was deteriorating, giving him permission to use the cabin of the boat (including a toilet) and its tender dinghy to get ashore. Brian spent several nights aboard Jeanne D'Arc which was owned coincidently by Lieutenant General Sir Frederick Browning and his wife Daphne du Maurier. Brian received a message from Mrs Wingfield-Digby to say that she was sending another crew member to help him continue the journey. An elderly inexperienced sailor arrived named Arnold Wright and Fortunette continued to sail east, however the inexperienced crew found themselves slightly overwhelmed by the wind and the little boat nearly capsized! They made it to the safety of the Yealm River which Arnold knew well as he lived in Noss Mayo. After being boarded by customs officers in Newton Ferrers, they moored Fortunette at the bottom of Arnold's garden at Myrtle Cottage where Brian remembered his wife cooked 'the nicest chips he had ever tasted.' Brian learned quickly how important it was to consider the wind strength and the tide, but this journey was to become his initiation into small yacht cruising which he enjoyed throughout his lifetime.

Marian would not reveal to Brian who any of his esteemed passengers had been back in the late 1940s when was working as a chauffeur and reminded him that he had signed the UK's Official Secrets Act.[45] Signing this legal document would have meant that Marian was legally bound not to share any sensitive information about his employer. Even when Brian pressed him on this, he would not reveal any details as to whom the passengers were over 40 years later, showing his dedication to his work and his conscientious nature.

---

44 Jeanne D'Arc was designed by Frederic A Fenger. The yacht had a wishbone rig. Fenger was interested in rigs that were manageable when sailing with limited crew.

45 The legislation governing the original alimentary Act of 1989 has seen several amendments. The relevant Act at this time would have been the Official Secrets Act of 1939. This has since been replaced by the Act of 1989.

Fortunette moored next to Jeanne D'Arc

Whilst he was working in this role at Milton Hall Marian made an application to live in Canada. Many Polish exiles relocated to Canada after the end of the war. Marian was hopeful of starting a new life after his very eventful start and as he had no family connections, this new adventure must have appealed to him, but he said in a dispirited tone on the tape that he had failed his medical test.

Marian became very unwell while he was working for the Fitzwilliam family and explained to Brian how he had discovered blood in his urine. The injuries that he had sustained during his parachute drop into Arnhem caused him yet another episode of distress. He had survived so much, which must have left him feeling very low. He remembered how he had taken himself off to the local pub one evening and tried to drown his sorrows by drinking beer, but it did not do him any good as he became seriously ill, and his employer called his own personal doctor to his bedside.

Marian was subsequently admitted to the Peterborough War Memorial Hospital where following an X-ray it was discovered that Marian had shrapnel embedded in his kidney. He underwent surgery so that it could be removed. This could well have been why Marian and Brian might have started chatting to one another in the first place, in their beds in Bournemouth Hospital, as Brian also had one kidney removed in 1970. He was diagnosed with an infection caused by tuberculosis that was due to being fed contaminated milk when he was a baby. His illness had developed suddenly, not many years after he was married and was a young father to myself and my sister Andrea.

After Marian recovered from his surgery he was still employed as a chauffeur but when the Labour Prime Minister, Clement Attlee came to power in October 1951, ex-Polish soldiers living in England were given permission to work in whatever job they wanted. Marian tried out several different jobs including hospitality work in the Randolph Hotel in Oxford and for a short while as an undertaker, which Marian referred to as a body snatcher! Feeling well again after recovering from the removal of his kidney, he found a job that suited him the best in the building trade, returning to the work that he had done for a short while before joining the Polish Army back in 1938. It was this change of circumstances that resulted in him moving to Bournemouth and finding a companion who he later married. Marian became a naturalised citizen of the UK in 1964 (see image on page 120).

During 1980 Marian revisited the spot from where he had made his daring escape from the St Elizabeth Hospital in Arnhem in 1944, as an injured soldier. He made an appeal in a local newspaper for the young Dutchman, who had helped him, to come forward. Contained in Brian's blue folder along with the cassette tapes was a photocopy of this newspaper article which was written in Dutch. Something I presume Marian had given him. The page title was 'Around the Rhine'.

> *Apt. Section Hayes* N.229
>
> **HOME OFFICE**
> NATIONALITY DIVISION
> Princeton House, 271 High Holborn, LONDON W.C.1
> Telephone: CHAncery 8811
>
> Please address any reply to
> THE UNDER SECRETARY
> OF STATE
> and quote: R.68445
> Your reference:
>
> 27 JUL 1964
>
> The Under Secretary of State presents his compliments and begs to say that the undermentioned person has been naturalised as a citizen of the United Kingdom and Colonies:
>
> Name MARIAN JOHN ROGUSKI
>
> Service No. 300 70 343
>
> Rank (if discharged - last rank held) PRIVATE
>
> Date and place of birth 11.2.1922. WARSAW, POLAND
>
> Former Nationality POLISH
>
> Granted Certificate of Naturalisation No. BNA 81067
>
> Effective date of Certificate of Naturalisation
> 1st JULY 1964
>
> The Officer-in-Charge , *Polish Records.*

I gave the article to a Dutch friend, who translated it for me as follows:

Who Helped the Polish Para?

Who has during the Battle of Arnhem met the Polish Paratrooper Marion Roguski? Who may have helped him when he was injured?

Roguski beat all the odds. He is still alive. He adopted British citizenship and now lives in Bournemouth on the south coast. At the latter stages of his life, he is suffering with severe disabilities. If he can prove out that these disabilities were because of his role in the Battle of Arnhem, as a paratrooper in service of the British Army, he could benefit from a British war pension, and this is why we are telling his story.

Roguski tells us the following:

'I was part of the First Polish Parachute regiment of the British Army and landed as a paratrooper in the area of Arnhem/Oosterbeek on 20/21 September 1944. During the battle I got injured on the shoulders and the back and was treated at the St Elizabeth Hospital (St Elizabeth Gasthuis). Shortly after the army had withdrawn and the enemy was close to reaching this place, I managed to escape to make my way to the riverbank. That must have been around the 10th October 1944.

Swimming

When I go to the riverbank, I met a young Dutch fellow of approximately 25 years of age. 178cm tall, and he had dark hair. This man became my friend. He pointed me to a safe place to cross the river swimming. He also helped me treating and bandaging my injuries.

This story was also told to Mr E.W. Ruston, an Englishman who is a volunteer with the British War Pension Service. Mr Ruston has written about this case to the Dutch mayor Mr Drijber. In this letter he stresses the importance of finding the Dutchman who treated the injuries of the paratrooper, as this would mean finding an important witness to Mr Roguski getting wounded during the Battle of Arnhem, on active duty with the British Army. On the other hand, Mr Roguski could have been injured in 1939, when he was on active duty for the Polish Army, in which case he would need to get this pension from Poland.

Pilgrimage

In the letter to the Dutch Mayor, Major Rushton furthermore mentioned: 'I pray and hope that you will be able to help us succeed in not only finding the Dutch man in question, but also in obtaining a war pension for Mr Roguski'. Last year he and his wife made their annual pilgrimage to Arnhem. They told us that – according to the letter to Mr Drijber – they were overwhelmed with friendly gestures from inhabitants of the city. In particular, they mentioned a Mrs. Steinweg ten Horn, Kerkweg 18, in Helium, who hopefully is also unabatedly continuing her search for the Dutch man.

Lately also the Arnhem council Information department has involved themselves. Any person with further information in their case can write to: Mr. Thomas Notermans. His contact details are as follows: Informationcentrum gemeente Arnhem, Beekstraat 62, 5811 DW Arnhem. His telephone number: 085-45711 extension 2797.

Translated by Erik Ritsema

Marian sitting on wall

It appears that Major Rushton was trying to help Marian prove that he had some entitlement to a British war pension as also contained within Brian's blue folder were two typewritten statements. One was written by a EW Rushton in 1982 and the other paper was a copy of a signed and sealed typewritten document stamped with the date 6 April 1982 in Amsterdam.

Dr Ribbers, a notary of Arnhem, signed this statement to officially record that a man had come forward, claiming to be the Dutch soldier who had helped Marian cross the Rhine back in 1944. This man was Mr Jannes Jan Dassen born in Rotterdam on 2 July in 1924. The statement reads as follows:

When the Battle of Arnhem (Operation Market Garden) began on the seventeenth of September One thousand and nine hundred and forty-four I was living in Arnhem. I was with the first aid service of the Dutch Red Cross. Together with other Red Cross People I was asked as a volunteer to give help to civilian casualties of this battle close as possible behind the fighting line. I was also to make efforts to restore the uninterrupted communication between the aid stations. I was on my bicycle heavily loaded with wound-dressing requirements and wore a Red Cross overall and a helmet.

At a certain moment the Paras were driven back by the Germans via Onderlangs and Utrechtseweg from Arnhem into the direction of Oosterbeek. The Elizabeth Hospital onto Utrechtseweg was occupied again by the Germans and used a dressing station for their wounded. In the Elizabeth Hospital wounded paras with orderlies had been left behind in forced captivity. When I passed the Elizabeth Hospital, I witnessed a partially successful flight of paras from this hospital. A small part of this group went into the direction of the centre of Arnhem and was captured by a group of Germans after one hundred and fifty meters and transported further into Arnhem. The largest part of the group crossed the street and fled into the plantation present there; they so escaped the notice of the guards present before the Elizabeth Hospital. They fled further helped by civilians that had stayed their houses and went into the direction of Oosterbeek.

On my further way that led over the completely deserted Klingelbeekseweg I arrived at a fairly large building situated in the centre of a large walled garden. Going along this wall that has been partially destroyed, my attention was drawn by a sound-signal (whistling through the teeth). It came from the bushes in the garden. Going in there I met two Polish Paras (one wounded, the other not) and one British Para. They told me they had escaped from the Elizabeth hospital. The wounded Pole had a wound in his upper leg, the wound must be dressed again. Then the Poles asked me to come with them to a back corner of the garden. There I met a Polish Para who was rather seriously wounded. The not wounded Pole told me that this Para also escaped from the Elizabeth Hospital. During the flight the dressing had moved and the wound had started to bleed again. The para was wounded in his right shoulder, back, hip and upper buttocks by shell-splinters. The largest wound had been coarsely stitched. One of the stitches was torn at one side. On my question he told me the stitches had been made by a German doctor in the Elizabeth hospital but he had not been examined medically for splinters still present. While I did the dressing the Pole said that the other wounded Pole were going to try and swim the river Rhine in the night to join the Poles, that according to him were on the other side of the river. I thought this impossible in view of his wounds.

At this moment aeroplanes of the Royal Air Force flew over to drop supplies. It was a pity that most of the containers landed in the German lines. One very low flying plane was hit by German flak (anti-aircraft guns). One of the engines stalled and caught fire. The plane made a curve of one hundred and eighty degrees. It went dropping supplies. Some people with parachutes sprang out and then the burning plane made belly landing in the low meadow west of the garden. Two men escaped and ran from the burning wreck and ran to a brick yard close by. From this brick yard a civilian ran towards after which three of them disappeared into the row of houses. Because the smoke of the burning wrecked plane was so thick, they went unseen by the Germans that were a. o. on the railway dike. I had understood meanwhile that the neighbours had gone to the brick yard for safety during the battle. After speaking with the Paras and having hidden by bicycle in the bushes I went to the brickyard with a bag of wound-dressing material. At the outer side of the garden wall a rivulet ran from the street side as in trench to the lower lying ground and further on to the river Rhine. An excellent natural covering through which I could reach the brick yard. I looked after some wounded people there. Then two Dutchmen came with me into the garden.

After consultation they were prepared to help the two wounded Poles further in their flight. The English wanted to go and try in the direction of Oosterbeek. The man who took care of the so seriously wounded Pole had black hair and was back in his twenties. Probably a Jew gone underground. After having given them dressing material for the two wounded Paras for the road we said goodbye and I went on my way along the Klingelbeekseweg into the direction of Oosterbeek.

Years after the Battle of Arnhem in the September Days when the daily papers are full of reports on commemorations of this battle, my thoughts went often to the two wounded Polish Paras. Did they make it? I did not give the Pole with the wounds in his back chance. Now, thirty-eight years after the Battle of Arnhem, I open the Nieuwe Krant of 26th February 1982 and I see the face of a soldier, whose face I have never forgotten: the Polish Para with the wounds in his back. No doubt whatsoever. He did make it then! What courage and stamina this man must have to swim the river Rhine back in one thousand nine hundred and forty-four, when he was so seriously wounded.

I know his name now from the paper: M. Roguski. I congratulate Mr Roguski with his success of that time and I wish him every success in getting a war pension. I thank Mr Roguski for his courageous part in our liberation and send him my best wishes for his further life.

Finally, the appearer declared to affirm the aforesaid by taking the oath before me, Notary. The appearer is known to me...............Notary. Instrument of which passed a single copy at Arnhem on the date mentioned in the preamble of the presents in the presence of the ladies Joke Tine Beerntsen-Mensink, secretary, residing at Arnhem and Agatha Klara Johanna Venverloo-Van Steenderen, notary's clerk residing in Dieren as witnesses.

After the appearer was informed of the substance of this instrument and upon full reading out this instrument is by the appearer, the witnesses and me, Notary. Sgd. J.J. Dassen, J.T. Beerntsen-Mensink, A.K.J. Venverloo-van, A.E. Ribbers.

I, the undersigned, Jeanette Grüdermann A.I.L, sworn translatrix of Arnhem, the Netherlands, do hereby CERTIFY that the foregoing English text is a full, true and faithful translation made of the document in Dutch. Witness, my hand this sixth day of April 1982. (And his signature below)

It must have been a very emotional visit for Marian to return to Arnhem, and to make connection with the man who had helped him when he was injured back in 1944. It also helps to explain the length of time Marian was in the St Elizabeth Hospital before he made his escape out of the window. Patients were permitted by the Germans to be treated at the hospital until the second week in October 1944 under the care of the British and Dutch medics.

CHAPTER 6

In 1995, when Marian met Brian in Bournemouth Hospital, he was tired, weary and sick. He was exhausted, not only from the physical demands on his life, but also from the bureaucratic system that prevented him from being recognised as a conscientious soldier, who should have been entitled to a war pension. He might have thought that Dad was his last hope that he was finally going to help him.

Dad kept in contact with Marian and his wife for several years. There were several letters in the blue folder from them, and although Marian's health was declining, they always sounded grateful for Dad's interest in Marian's wartime life. Marian died four years later in 1998 in Bournemouth, and his widow died in 2002. Dad, I believe was not even aware that they had died, and when he did find out, he kept his thoughts to himself. I think he perhaps considered that he should have done more to help his friend and mentioned several times to me and my daughters that he had some incredible stories that needed to be written about. We brushed off these comments as we had our own lives to live, so the tapes and Marian's life story were tucked away in a corner of Woodbine Cottage, until they were discovered in 2021.

The Long Walk: The True Story of a Trek to Freedom by Slavomir Rawicz was published in 1965. Rawicz, a young Polish calvary officer, seven years older than Marian, claimed that he and six others had escaped from a Siberian gulag camp in 1941. The book is an account of their journey, which crossed the Trans-Siberian Railway before travelling south into Tibet, crossing the Gobi Desert before arriving in India in March 1942.

On 30 October 2006, a documentary was broadcast on BBC Radio 4 FM presented by Tim Whewell. The documentary producer Hugh Levinson and his researchers had set out to discover if Rawicz's account was true and it caused a lot of controversy at the time. Rawicz could not produce any evidence to support his story, and parts of his tales were proven to be untrue. Rawicz was a serving Polish serviceman but had claimed that he had escaped in 1941, yet Soviet records showed that he had been released in 1942. Another researcher, Linda Willis, who was researching the book, discovered documents that revealed Rawicz was released from a gulag camp in 1942 as part of the amnesty for Polish soldiers in Soviet territory.

In 2009 another ex-Polish serviceman, Witold Glinski, claimed that Rawicz had stolen his own story, and used it to publish the book. Both men's accounts were exciting and enthralling, but neither could be completely proven, so the controversy over the authenticity of the story caused much debate amongst researchers. However, the book became an international bestseller and sold millions of copies. Factually, thousands of soldiers did find themselves having to survive the conditions of the Siberian terrain, even if they were prisoners or not and many different accounts of how they managed to survive have been written or recounted to relatives. Stalin did release Polish prisoners in 1942 but he did not help them with transport, so they would have been trapped in the location of their imprisonment, many of which were in Siberia. Some rejoined General Anders' Army and become part of a larger group, but there were men who made their own way and survived in very unbelievable circumstances.

In the online comments section of a BBC article about the Radio 4 documentary written by Levinson there are many testimonies to relatives who had undertaken similar long and harsh journeys, such as Feliks Krzewinski, whose paintings recording his memories are displayed in the Imperial War Museum. Other comments relating to this article, posted from relatives of Polish survivors, ask why Rawicz's account needed to be challenged, when all accounts of Polish soldiers making these astonishing journeys were valuable to society, in helping to understand the horrors of survival under Stalin's brutal regime. For example, Szymon from Newcastle, wrote 'Why is it necessary to question the validity of such stories so closely? Why does there have to be such a burden of proof?' Szymon's statement was reassuring to me, as the only information that remains about Marian's journey is his recorded voice, on my dad's Dictaphone tapes. For me, there has been so much to gain from listening to this voice, other than trying to prove the accuracy of his memory. The historical education has been immense.

It is possible that Marian read *The Long Walk* and might have used some of the details from it to fabricate his own memories to recount to Brian, but all the Polish servicemen who were captured by the Soviets in 1939 experienced an extremely frightening and difficult time in captivity. None were given any form of transportation, when they were released by Stalin in 1942, yet many soldiers found their way to Syria and India to rejoin the Polish Army. The details that Marian shared with Brian in hospital were an intimate insight into the early years of a young man who had no other choice than to try to survive.

The higher-ranking Polish officers who survived such as Czapski, were educated which gave them the skills to write accounts of their time in captivity after World War Two. It is less likely that soldiers such as Marian possessed the type of skills needed to record their experiences, and with no access to military pensions the focus of their lives would have continued to be about survival. You can understand why Rawicz took the opportunity to publish *The Long Walk,* to an audience in 1956, in a bid to cash in on his miserable early life with an enhanced version of actual events.

Marian was tired and ill when he told his life story to Brian, so it is undoubtedly a blurred recollection of events. Nonetheless, this version is all we have, and writing it has been humbling.

A Polish Voice

A Polish Voice

Deported to USSR in 1940. Joined the Polish Forces in USSR on 10.2.1942. Crossing the Soviet-Iranian border with his unit, came under British command as above. Served in the Middle East when transferred to the United Kingdom. Arrived on 16.10.1942 and posted to the Polish Independent Parachute Brigade. Took part in the Airborne operation code-named "MARKET GARDEN" at Arnhem and Driel, Holland 18.9.44-12.10.44. Served on the Continent as part of the British Forces of Occupation of Germany 13.5.45-31.3.47.

Medals and Awards:
    Polish: Field Parachute Badge, Army Medal
    British: France and Germany, Defence Medal (CS20 and PSF46(R) enclosed)

Conduct: Good

Remarks: If it is necessary for you to submit this statement to a third party for any purpose you should take such action as will ensure its return to your custody.

A Polish Voice

A conference took place in 1945 in the Black Sea resort of Yalta, now in Ukraine, between the UK Prime Minister Churchill, US President Roosevelt and the Soviet Premiere Stalin. This meeting was primarily arranged to discuss how the defeated Germany would be organised at the end of the war. Decisions were made about the division of territories and Poland became under the Soviet Union's domination. A new communist government was formed in Poland, which was recognised by Great Britain instead of the exiled Polish government. Many of the military forces who were based in the UK had been loyal to the exiled government and found themselves with a very unsettling future, when the countries they had left before the beginning of the war had been annexed by the Soviet Union. Arguments over which Polish forces should attend the parade in London, led to all the invitations being declined.

An official British Victory Parade was held on 8 June 1946, in London, to mark the end of the war. However, despite the Allied forces being represented in the parade, the Polish military were not permitted to take part which is staggering! In 2003 Prime Minister Tony Blair requested that Polish forces be represented at a 60th Anniversary Commemorative event planned in London in 2005 after issuing an apology for them not being included in the original parade.

The Poles led the march along The Mall.

MEMORIALS

Whilst this book is written as memorial to Brian and Marian, many of the others mentioned have memorials dedicated to them:

When the bodies of Polish officers were found in the Katyn Forest near Smolensk in 1943, German leaders gave the Polish Red Cross permission for a cemetery to be built but when the area fell back under Soviet control it was destroyed. After the war the Soviet Union made efforts to block the Polish community from creating a memorial in London by putting pressure on the British government. They did not want the victims of Katyn to be commemorated. In 1979 a monument in Gunnersbury Cemetery in Chiswick was erected and dedicated, but without any representation from the British government. Soviet leader, Mikhail Gorbachev, officially accepted blame for the country's crime in 1990, allowing archaeologists to work in the forest and the exhumation of human remains to be carried out.[46] The Cemetery to the Victims of Totalitarianism was opened in Kharkiv on 17 June 2000 with both the Polish and the Ukrainian Prime Ministers in attendance and a large war cemetery constructed in the Katyn Forest, near Smolensk in Russia, was opened on 28 July 2000 and attended by the Polish Prime Minister, Jerzy Buzek and the Russian Interior Minister, Vladimir Rushailo.

During this same year war cemeteries opened at the sites of other mass murders, in Mednoye, Russia and at Piatykhatky near Kharkiv, Ukraine.

---

46 Exhumation and sampling work that began in 1991 at Katyn, Mednoye and Kharkiv where the bodies of Polish prisoners of war from NKVD camps Kozelsk, Starobilsk and Ostashkov were found continued over many years. The independent Historical Committee for Investigation into the Katyn Massacre published cemetery record books. The Ministry of Culture and National Heritage of Poland have now made these records available to the public in digital form and with advances in the knowledge relating to the massacre's identification of many of the individuals has been possible.

Family members of those killed in the Katyn Massacre were travelling to Smolensk in April 2010 to attend a commemoration event along with senior Polish dignitaries and clergy members. The Polish Air Force aeroplane they were travelling in crashed, killing all of the 96 passengers aboard. Again, as in the case of Sikorski's 1943 plane crash, investigations found nothing wrong with the aircraft and foggy weather conditions were blamed for the crash leading to more conspiracy theories about political assassination.

A memorial complex was created on the outskirts of Kharkiv, known as the Lisopark neighbourhood. An area that was formerly a forest in the 1930s became inhabited due to the expansion of a nuclear research facility. The mass burial site was discovered by children playing in woods near their homes, as they found skulls, buttons and uniform insignias in the ground. They took these items into school but initially links to a burial site were dismissed by their teachers. When Ukraine became an independent state on 1 August 1991 the government admitted that the area was a burial site of Polish officers in 1940 and of Soviet citizens who had been executed by Stalin's regime in 1937–8. Another memorial site in Ukraine was established in 1994 where a village called Bykivnia had existed during Stalin's rule. A national monument was erected here in 2006 in the woodland to honour the memory of the estimated 200,000 people who were buried there in mass graves including 3,435 Polish officers captured by the Soviet Red Army in 1939. In 2012 this became the fourth Polish war cemetery associated with the Katyn Massacre.

A human rights organisation in Ukraine reported on 8 May 2020, the same day that Brian died, which also coincided with the 75th anniversary of World War Two, that Russian officials had removed memorial plaques, erected in 1991, on a former NKVD building in Tver, Russia. One of the plaques had the following inscription: *'In remembrance of the Poles from the Ostashkov Camp, murdered by the NKVD in Kalinin. As a warning to the world'.*[lii] The author of the report claimed that President Vladimir Putin is keen to blur these parts of

Soviet history, and these actions show that Russia continues to deny the historical truth.

Many of the UK's VE Day 2020 celebrations were cancelled due to the Covid pandemic, including the 75th anniversary parade events in London. Brian's long life also came to an end on 8 May as he died in Dorchester Hospital aged 85. It was a glorious sunny day with hundreds of flags flying in remembrance of all those who had died in World War Two.

A monument was unveiled in 1989 on the banks of the River Rhine which commemorates 'Operation Berlin', the nighttime evacuation of paratroopers involved in Operation Market Garden in 1944. It is located on the site of the evacuation route at Drielse Rijndijk, Driel. On a black marble panel is the following inscription: '… *they were just whispers and shadows in the night …* ' and an information panel beside the memorial reads: *'It is 25th September 1944, The battle of Arnhem is still raging, but the position of the surrounded British and Polish Airborne troops on the northern Rhine bank has become untenable. Then the order for their evacuation across the river is given. In that rainy night hundreds of soldiers come in small parties to the river forelands both clearly visible from here and wait to be rescued. Under heavy German fire from the Westerbouwing British and Canadian Engineers make dozens of trips in their small boats from this bank. In one night, supported by other units they manage to rescue 2,400 Airborne troops. At the same time the rescue had hardly seen their savers, so they have never been able to thank them. This monument has been erected to express their gratitude (15th September 1989).'*

The soldiers who were killed serving with the 4th and 5th Battalions of the Dorset Regiment have a monument and a terrace dedicated to them at the Westerbouwing restaurant near Oosterbeek.

A memorial was unveiled in 2006 in Driel, dedicated to Major General Sosabowski and in London a blue memorial plaque was put up in 2012 at 2 St Georges Road, Chiswick which was where he lived from 1950 to 1960. He is buried in Warsaw, Poland.

Two memorials are dedicated to Joe Eugene Mann of the 502nd Parachute Infantry Regiment, part of the 101st Airborne Division. Joe was killed in 1944 in Operation Market Garden shielding his comrades with his body from the blast of a hand grenade, for which he was awarded the United States Military's Medal of Honour. The monument is near an open-air theatre and was designed to represent a mythical story of a pelican sacrificing her own flesh and blood to protect its young. The other monument is close to the spot where he died at the bridge at Best.

Lipmann-Kessel was buried in Oosterbeek in 1986 at his own request near the soldiers who died in Operation Market Garden.

General Sikorski's body was transferred by boat and train from Gibraltar to Westminster Cathedral for a funeral service on 15 July 1943, that was attended by 3,000 people including Churchill. He was buried the following day in a Polish war cemetery in Newark-on-Trent in Nottinghamshire, but he was exhumed and repatriated to Krakow 50 years after his death. There is also a memorial dedicated to him, and other passengers who died in the plane crash including his daughter, in Gibraltar.

A bust of General Anders was unveiled in 2021 in London's National Army Museum and there is another in the Polish Army Museum in Warsaw. He died in London in 1970 and after his body had laid in state he was buried with fallen soldiers he had commanded, at the Polish war cemetery at Monte Cassino in Italy, as he had requested.

Lieutenant General Horrocks died in 1985 and a memorial service was held for him in Westminster Abbey. After his cremation his ashes were left unclaimed at an undertaker's chapel of rest near Chichester. The Royal British Legion tracked down his grandchildren and in 2022 they were interned at St Paul's Church in Mill Hill, London during a full military service. The actor Edward Fox who played his part in the film *A Bridge Too Far* attended the service.

CONCLUSION

Whilst researching and writing this book I have learnt that a person's voice is a far more intimate connection to their memory than photographs are. I have both printed and digital photographs of my dad, and film recordings too, and these will all be treasured. I never met Marian, as I have only been left his voice and a few other items. I learnt about his life purely from listening to the recordings and researching what he said but in hearing his gentle voice on the tapes, he now feels very familiar to me, so I have sort of got to know him posthumously because my dad took time in the hospital to listen and record his voice.

In the blue folder that contained the tape recordings there was also one colour photograph of Brian and Marian sitting beside one another on the bed in Bournemouth Hospital.

Dad and Marian

There was also the photocopied article from a Dutch magazine, that was folded and rather creased. At some point it had become damp and was stuck together in parts. Unfortunately, it was the picture in the article that had stuck the most and as I eased it apart, the image tore badly. Looking at the edges that were left, I could tell that it was a picture of Marian in uniform, probably taken when he was still a Polish soldier. I could not see his face and that made me feel a little sad, as I have developed a fond connection with him after listening to his voice regularly. Listening to my own father's voice on the tapes did not make me feel mournful. I have recordings that were made later in his life, which have more of an emotional effect on me. The man who is speaking on the Dictaphone tapes was my younger dad, not the one who became frail and confused in his later years. I enjoyed hearing his younger voice, it brought back happy memories for me.

A chance meeting in Bournemouth Hospital during 1995 brought Brian and Marian together and their connection and subsequent friendship may well have been initiated during a conversation that revealed that they had both experienced an operation to have one kidney removed.

Brian was in awe of Marian; otherwise, why would he have taken the time to go back and record his story on his Dictaphone? Brian's enthusiasm and effort to record Marian's life story was, I believe, because of the respect that he held, throughout his life, for Polish people. His childhood was deeply affected by events associated with World War Two. Brian met a man in Bournemouth Hospital who had a very difficult life, a Polish soldier who had survived when so many had perished and he understood the pain this man had endured, not just personally, but completely as a Polish citizen. Dad didn't write the story about Marian's life because he had too many other things that he wanted to do in his own life, and writing a book wasn't really in his remit. So, I have written it instead, and I have dedicated it to Brian's four grandchildren, who he loved dearly, because I want them to remember him, and I want them to know that his life shaped theirs and hopefully they will listen to others in the same way that he did.

Brian and Marian both used humour in their post-war lives as a defence from the evil things that they knew had happened at the hands of Hitler and Stalin. They could not unknow things that became atrocious historical facts, that are now studied as part of school curriculums. Brian was grateful for his peacetime life but Marian, being 13 years older, was becoming a frail aged man when they met on the ward, and in seeing this decline, it probably reminded Brian of his own mortality. I believe both of them understood how fortunate they were to live without the fear of tyranny. He never spoke much about the war to me as a child, and if he did it would always be a humorous story, he would never talk about anything that would upset or frighten me. Even when my own daughters were learning about the Holocaust as part of their schoolwork, he was not keen to discuss those years with them either. It was only later in his eighties that he began to want to talk about the event that he had witnessed on his way to school in 1940.

I very nearly did not complete this book; I nearly gave up as the research enquiries I submitted to the Ministry of Defence took eight months to arrive and during that time I became doubtful that I would be able to prove that Marian had served as a Polish soldier, so I was delighted when I received his military service records.

In Chapter 2 I wrote about the Eveny people who live with the reindeer in Siberia. Shamanism, the religion that is part of their culture, teaches that the spirituality of a deceased person flows through those who are alive now. I feel grateful to be able do the same thing by writing this book.

I have been humbled learning about the passionate people of Poland who took on the might of Nazi terror in the Warsaw Uprising, the Czech and the Dutch citizens who took great risks with their own lives in order to save others and the thousands of Polish people who were murdered at the hands of the dictators, Hitler and Stalin. If this little book encourages a few more people to learn about the histories of war, and why atrocities happen, then Marian's life is an important legacy for the future. When Aleksandr Solzhenitsyn eventually finished writing the epic book *The Gulag Archipelago* he stated in the epilogue that he could not fully understand why he should write the book, but he understood that as all the information that he had gathered from prisoners of the gulags had been given to him, then for that reason alone he thought that he should do it. I am of the same opinion as Solzhenitsyn, I was given the information about Marian, so therefore I felt the need to write it down. Proving Marian's involvement with Operation Market Garden gave me the greatest gratification. On the wall of the Museum Hartenstein, formerly the hotel in Oosterbeek near Arnhem that was used as the Airborne headquarters there is a sign that reads:

'If in the years to come any man says to you "I fought at Arnhem", take off your hat to him and buy him drink, for this is the stuff of which England's greatness is made.'

War correspondent Alan Wood in the Daily Express,
24 September 1944.

References

i	Beevor: 40, 2018	xliv	Lipmann-Kessel: 13, 1976
ii	Dowell: 2019 https://www.thefirstnews.com/article/lesser-known-horror-of-stalins-great-purge-which-saw-over-100k-poles-massacred-goes-on-display-in-harrowing-new-exhibition-7565	xlv	Lipmann-Kessel: 58, 1976
		xlvi	Beevor: 21, 2018
		xlvii	Salverda: 103, 2016
		xlviii	Lipmann-Kessel: 44, 1976
		xlix	Watt: 3, 1989
iii	Cholewczynski: 31, 1993	l	Van der Zee: 158, 1982
iv	Applebaum: 516, 2003	li	Watt: 3, 1989
v	Vilensky: x, 1999	lii	Coynash: Kharkiv Human Rights Protection Group 8 May 2020
vi	Taylor: 1972		
vii	Solzhenitsyn: Part 2 – The Slave Caravans, 2003		
viii	Wiciak: 4, 2018		
ix	Snyder: viii, 2018		
x	Karpeles: xxxi, 2018		
xi	Karpeles: xiii, 2018		
xii	Karpeles: xx, 2018		
xiii	Rogoyska: 20–1, 2021		
xiv	Ambros: 2002		
xv	Rogoyska: 58, 2021		
xvi	Rawicz: 53, 1956		
xvii	Cienciala et al: 289, 2007		
xviii	Cienciala et al: 301, 2007		
xix	Rogoyska: 146, 2021		
xx	Rogoyska: 302, 2021		
xxi	Sturcke: The Guardian 29 January 2009		
xxii	Beevor: 40–1, 2018		
xxiii	Beevor: 314, 2018		
xxiv	Beevor: 14, 2018		
xxv	Sosabowski: 142, 2013		
xxvi	Beevor: 269, 2018		
xxvii	Beevor: 75, 2018		
xxviii	Beevor: 148, 2018		
xxix	Sosabowski: 147, 2013		
xxx	Beevor: 86, 2018		
xxxi	Beevor: 81, 2018		
xxxii	Beevor: 245, 2018		
xxxiii	Beevor: 246, 2018		
xxxiv	Cholewczynski: 129, 1993		
xxxv	Cholewczynski: 161, 1993		
xxxvi	Cholewczynski: 200, 1993		
xxxvii	The Pegasus Archive		
xxxviii	Beevor: 326, 2018		
xxxix	Beevor: 332, 2018		
xl	Beevor: 338, 2018		
xli	Lipmann-Kessel: 13, 1976		
xlii	Hackett: 25, 1977		
xliii	Hackett: 24, 1977		

Bibliography

A Journey of a Polish Soldier – Michelle Wiciak. Independently Published, Kindle, 2018.

Arnhem: The Battle for the Bridges, 1944 – Antony Beevor. Viking, 2018.

Chapter from *Discord and Consensus in the Low Countries, 1700-2000. Beyond A Bridge Too Far: the aftermath of the Battle of Arnhem (1944) and its Impact on Civilian Life* – Reinier Salverda. UCL Press, 2016.

Coynash, H. 'Russian removes memorial to Katyn Massacre in new attack on historical truth'. Kharkiv Human Rights Protection Group Online 2020.

Freely I Served: The Memoir of Commander – 1st Polish Independent Parachute Brigade 1941-1944 – Major General Stanislaw Sosabowski. Pen & Sword Books, 2013.

Gulag – Anne Applebaum. Kindle, Bantam Doubleday Dell Publishing Group, 2003.

How War Came: The Immediate Origins of the Second World War 1938-1939 – Donald Cameron Watt. William Heinemann Ltd, 1989.

I was a Stranger – General Sir John Hackett. Chatto & Windus, 1977.

Inhuman Land: Searching for the Truth in Soviet Russia 1941-1942 – Józef Czapski. New York Review of Books, 2018.

Inhuman Land: Searching for the Truth in Soviet Russia 1941-1942. Introduction – Timothy Snyder. New York Review of Books, 2018.

Katyn: A Crime Without Punishment – Edited by Anna M Cienciala, Natalia S Lebedeva and Wojciech Materski. Yale University Press, 2007.

Looking for Mr. Smith: A Quest for the Truth Behind The Long Walk, the Greatest Survival Story Ever Told – Linda Willis. Skyhorse Publishing, 2010.

Lost Time Lectures on Proust in a Soviet Prison Camp – Józef Czapski (Translated by Eric Karpeles) New York Review of Books, 2018.

Island: Nijmegen to Arnhem – Tim Saunders. Leo Cooper, 2002.
Poles Apart – George F Cholewczynski. Sarpedon Publishers Inc, 1993.
Stolen Childhood: A Saga of Polish War Children – Lucjan Królikowski OFM Conv. Translated by Kazimierz J Rozniatowski. Author's Choice Press, 2001.
Sturcke, J. 'Tests on Poland's wartime leader debunk assassination theories, say investigators' *The Guardian* Online Newspaper, 2009.
Surgeon at Arms – Alexander Lipmann-Kessel. Leo Cooper, 1976.
Surviving Katyn – Jane Rogoyska. One World Publications, 2021.
The Brief Sun – Robert Ambros. Kindle AuthorHouse, 2002.
The Gulag Archipelago [Abridged] – Aleksandr Solzhenitsyn. Harvill Press, 2003.
The Gulag Handbook, an Encyclopedia Dictionary of Soviet Penitentiary Institutions and Terms Related to the Forced Labor Camps – Jacques Rossi Translated from Russian by William A Burhans. Paragon House, 1989.
The Hunger Winter: Occupied Holland 1944-5 – Henri van der Zee. Jill Norman & Hobhouse Ltd, 1982.
The Long Walk: The True Story of a Trek to Freedom – Slavomir Rawicz. The Lyons Press, 1997.
The Pegasus Archive – https://www.pegasusarchive.org
The Warsaw Uprising – George Bruce. Kindle – Sapere Books, 2021.
Till My Tale is Told – Edited by Simeon Vilensky. Virago Press, 1999.
Reindeer People: Living with Animals and Spirits in Siberia – Piers Vitebsky. HarperCollins, 2005.
White Eagle Red Star – Norman Davies. Foreword – AJP Taylor Macdonald and Co. 1972.